Consuming Crisis

Sara Miller McCune founded SAGE Publishing in 1965 to support the dissemination of usable knowledge and educate a global community. SAGE publishes more than 1000 journals and over 800 new books each year, spanning a wide range of subject areas. Our growing selection of library products includes archives, data, case studies and video. SAGE remains majority owned by our founder and after her lifetime will become owned by a charitable trust that secures the company's continued independence.

Los Angeles | London | New Delhi | Singapore | Washington DC | Melbourne

Consuming Crisis

Commodifying Care and COVID-19

Francesca Sobande

Los Angeles | London | New Delhi
Singapore | Washington DC | Melbourne

Los Angeles | London | New Delhi
Singapore | Washington DC | Melbourne

SAGE Publications Ltd
1 Oliver's Yard
55 City Road
London EC1Y 1SP

SAGE Publications Inc.
2455 Teller Road
Thousand Oaks, California 91320

SAGE Publications India Pvt Ltd
B 1/I 1 Mohan Cooperative Industrial Area
Mathura Road
New Delhi 110 044

SAGE Publications Asia-Pacific Pte Ltd
3 Church Street
#10-04 Samsung Hub
Singapore 049483

Editor: Delayna Spencer
Editorial assistant: Bali Birch-Lee
Production editor: Sarah Cooke
Marketing manager: Ruslana Khatagova
Cover design: Wendy Scott
Typeset by: C&M Digitals (P) Ltd, Chennai, India
Printed in the UK

Library of Congress Control Number: 00000000

British Library Cataloguing in Publication data

A catalogue record for this book is available
from the British Library

ISBN 978-1-5297-9397-0
ISBN 978-1-5297-9396-3 (pbk)

At SAGE we take sustainability seriously. Most of our products are printed in the UK using responsibly
sourced papers and boards. When we print overseas we ensure sustainable papers are used as
measured by the PREPS grading system. We undertake an annual audit to monitor our sustainability.

DEDICATION

This book is dedicated to my mum and dad. I love you.

This book is also dedicated to my grandparents, from whom I learnt much about care, candour, conviction, and comfort.

TABLE OF CONTENTS

ABOUT THE AUTHOR

Dr Francesca Sobande is a senior lecturer in digital media studies at the School of Journalism, Media and Culture (Cardiff University, Wales). She is the author of *The Digital Lives of Black Women in Britain* (Palgrave Macmillan, 2020), co-editor with Professor Akwugo Emejulu of *To Exist is to Resist: Black Feminism in Europe* (Pluto Press, 2019), and co-author with layla-roxanne hill of *Black Oot Here: Black Lives in Scotland* (Bloomsbury, 2022). Francesca's work particularly focuses on digital remix culture, Black diaspora and archives, feminism, creative work, pop culture, and devolved nations. She tweets at @chess_ess

ACKNOWLEDGEMENTS

The process of writing *Consuming Crisis: Commodifying Care and COVID-19* was made possible by many people, including loved ones who I grieved during that time, and whose words, wit, laughter, care, and presence will be forever felt.

I am particularly thankful for the guidance of Delayna Spencer (Senior Commissioning Editor, SAGE) who saw something in my work before the idea for this book was even formed. I vividly remember the first conversation we had which left me feeling inspired about the prospect of working together and was a reminder of what a joy writing can be.

From start to finish, I have been fully backed in my intention to write a book about care, consumer culture, and the COVID-19 crisis – and to write it in a way that draws on scholarly research, as well as reflexive and speculative writing. Delayna's unwavering encouragement included memorable moments of reassurance regarding the space and time away from this work that I needed while in the grips of grief. Essentially, this book would not exist without the ever-present support and generosity of those around me.

Thank you to Professor Jason Arday and Professor Meredith D. Clark for the helpful and supportive SAGE 'Social Science for Social Justice' series editorial feedback on *Consuming Crisis*. The generous and encouraging comments that were offered helped me to develop this book and the direction that it went in.

As always, to all who are (and were) (t)here – thank you / diolch.

PREFACE

I hate the word 'normal'.

Stating this may make me seem desperate to prove just how 'different' I am – in ways reminiscent of the memefied 'I'm weird …' speech by emo-esque character Jughead Jones in CW's *Riverdale*. However, the truth is that having a critical take on notions of 'normal' life is far from being something new or unique. Instead, my feelings about societal constructions of 'normality' are feelings that have been expressed by many people before me, and no doubt, will be articulated by many people for years to come.

As with all words, perceptions of what the word 'normal' means are shaped by 'shared conceptual maps' (Hall, 1997a, 1997b). Effectively, people's sense of what 'normal' means depends on societally shared ideas about language and life, including shifting impressions of who and what is and is not 'normal'. Put differently, without being able to anticipate who and what other people might deem to be 'normal', the concept of 'normal' as 'we' know it ceases to exist. Words become meaningful in ways that are innately social, and so, their meanings are always open to interpretation and contestation.

Still, in the rousing words of sociologist, cultural theorist, and political activist Stuart Hall (1997b: 9), 'if we shared no concepts together with other folks, we literally could not make sense of the world together'. That said, 'we all don't make sense of things in the same way … therefore each of us has a little kind of conceptual world of our own … or rather, we have our own sort of take on the conceptual world' (ibid.).

Media and political ponderings about an alleged return to 'normal' life became a defining feature of 2020–2022, a point in time that constitutes the (ongoing) COVID-19 (coronavirus) crisis. However, rarely have such ponderings involved critical consideration of the different, and, even conflicting, ways that people (and brands) interpret the notion of 'normal' life and what forms of care are (or are not) part of it. Moreover, although prior scholarly work has explored how constructions of 'care' circulate in the context of consumer culture and capitalism, few have examined the relationship between this and the raced, gendered, and classed concepts of so-called 'normal' life.

Intentionally and otherwise, much discourse on returning to 'normal' life between 2020–2022 has highlighted the very particular ideas, experiences, and people that are societally framed as acceptable, normal, and idealized in the United Kingdom (UK), as well as beyond it. Consequently, notions of 'normal' life that circulated within and across public spheres during these years also illuminated what sort of ideas, experiences, and people are regarded as undesirable, abnormal, and stigmatized 'Others' (Tyler, 2020). Such discourse on 'normal' life reveals much about constructions and experiences of care and comfort, including societal perceptions of who is 'worthy' of care and comfort (Ahmed, 2004; Johnson, 2020), who 'should' provide it, and what being cared for looks and feels like (Bailey and Mobley, 2018).

This book is based on a critical understanding of the loaded nature of the notion of 'normal' life in the UK, including how ideas about 'normality' and 'togetherness' are invoked in ways that reflect forms of structural oppression and promote specific socio-political perspectives which are repackaged as universal experiences. By focusing on the relationship and schism between care, commodification, and the COVID-19 crisis, I grapple with how notions of 'normal' life function as part of the porous and potent dynamics between people, profit, places, pandemics, and politics.

February 2022 – Dr. Francesca Sobande, Cardiff, Wales

1

WHOSE 'NEW NORMAL'?

Who and what is deemed to be 'normal', and who and what is framed as the contrasting 'Other'?

Who and what determines this, and why?

How are ideas about 'normal life' constructed in consumer culture during times of crisis?

NORMAL IS NOT A NEUTRAL CONCEPT

The days, months, and years before the COVID-19 (coronavirus) pandemic are often nostalgically referred to as being part of the 'normal life' that many people long to return to. Whose perceptions of 'normal life' are foregrounded in current discourse concerning crisis and a ('good') time before COVID? What does examining these matters reveal about experiences (and a lack) of care and comfort? These questions are at the core of this book, which examines elements of the UK's media and marketing landscape, including their entanglements with messages of empowerment, multiculturalism, and nationalism.

I explore how seemingly 'global' branding trends during the crisis (e.g., marketing messages of 'togetherness') have drawn on 'national cultural formations' (Hesse, 2000: 5) and invoked ideas about both care and productivity (Sobande, 2020a; Sobande and Klein, 2022).

If this book were a recipe, it would be two parts critical analysis of adverts, and two parts provocations concerning the concepts of care, comfort, normality, and angst. Effectively, this work is based on empirical analysis of key advertising examples (e.g., Boohoo, Deliveroo, Dettol, Halifax) and critical consideration of various online trends. This includes discussion of the idiosyncrasies of influencer culture, aspects of corporate communications in higher education, and the socio-political significance of the rise of home-baking and its beautified documentation on social media. However, the discussion that binds the book's ingredients together is also made up of reflections and ruminations that move beyond commenting on the content of adverts and the practices of brands. My inclusion of many moments of (self)reflection in this book is based on the perspective that '[r]eflection is not a departure from action. Instead, it is a precursor, or, perhaps, it is even action by another name' (Sobande and Emejulu, 2021: 2).

Across four dialogic chapters, I focus on the coronavirus pandemic and interconnected crises of capitalism, to explore the relationship between consumer culture, the politics and perceptions of care(lessness), and COVID-19. Throughout these pages, I blend analysis of content and communications with self-reflexive and speculative writing, to consider how various experiences have been (re)framed across media, marketplace, and political spheres. Thus, I expand on work about how '[t]he lockdown has made blatantly evident, in the vein of an old faithful class analysis, how different our homes are' (Degot and Riff, 2022: 13) – but I turn my attention to differences between constructions and experiences of care and so-called 'normal' life.

My analysis emerges from the fact that there was a care-related crisis in the UK long before the pandemic – from inadequate provision of mental health care to the persistence of medical racism (Linton and Walcott, 2022). As I and writer, curator, and organizer layla-roxanne hill (2022) argue in our book *Black Oot Here: Black Lives in Scotland*, 'stressful working and living environments impact significantly on well-being and mental health, particularly for those on low or no income and living in "deprived" areas' (78), and such inequalities cannot only be attributed to the impact of COVID-19 – but the crisis has, in some cases, exacerbated them.

This opening chapter sets the scene for careful consideration of the construction and commodification of care during this crisis, including my examination of different scholarly accounts of what constitutes care and its perceived (a)political underpinnings. Chapter 1 also outlines key concepts and work that informs my book, by addressing the following themes:

- Normal is not a neutral concept
- National culture, neoliberalism, and care
- The rhetoric of the COVID-19 crisis
- Racial capitalism and constructions of care and comfort

As may be apparent, I am prone to writing relatively long introductory chapters and I tend to '(over)use' parenthesis (more on this is covered in Chapter 3's discussion of distraction and dreaming...). I considered condensing Chapter 1 and resisting my impulse to add and share my thoughts in the ways that feel most natural (often, and partly because of my ADHD and 'brain fog', with the use of parenthesis!). However, the sentiments that stir this book include an intention to refuse pressures to (re)present ideas and thoughts in ways that betray the messy and always ongoing process that gives them life. Maybe that is a long-winded way of saying that I could not bring myself to abandon some of my stylistic inclinations, or to 'kill all my darlings'. In any case, this book is intended to be more inviting and engaging than rigidly structured or polished.

Informed by the work of Mukherjee and Banet-Weiser (2012: 1) on 'struggles over what social activism means', I reflect on what brands' positioning themselves in proximity to activism indicates concerning changing dynamics between commercial imperatives and social justice. In 2020, *The Wall Street Journal* asked, '[a]s the coronavirus pandemic progresses, companies are searching to find the right tone and message for their marketing. How are some of the world's most recognizable companies reenvisioning their advertising?'. Accordingly, I address questions such as the following:

- What concepts of care and constructions of comfort and camaraderie have been communicated through adverts amid the COVID-19 crisis?
- How have brands and the people who study them described the purpose of advertising, branding, and marketing in recent years?
- How are ideas about national culture, multiculturalism, and being a 'good citizen' implicated in marketing content in response to COVID-19?
- What discourses of home life and productivity have been a part of brand messaging during this time?

From Boohoo's (2022) celebratory 'HERE'S TO 2022, HERE'S TO YOU', to Deliveroo's (2021) patriotic 'England 'Til We Dine', I examine crucial examples of how brands have claimed to care during the COVID-19 crisis. In addition to critically considering how ineffective terms such as 'brand activism' have functioned, I scrutinize some of the many ways brands have sought to sustain their image during the COVID-19 crisis by (re)presenting themselves as 'one of us'. Attuned to how nation branding functions (Aronczyk, 2013; Jiménez-Martínez, 2021; Sobande and hill, 2022), I address who and what consist of the 'us' that brands present themselves as invested in (e.g., heroism, nationalism, patriotism, 'nuclear' families, heteronormative coupledom, #GirlBoss feminism, and marketable middle-class domesticity).

NATIONAL CULTURE, NEOLIBERALISM, AND CARE

My exploration of some of the narratives that brands have depended on during the COVID-19 crisis involves analysis that is informed by Black cultural studies and Black studies in Britain, including pivotal work on *Un/Settled Multiculturalisms* (Hesse, 2000), and writing on the work and labour experiences of Black people, such as the contributions of scholars Winston James and Clive Harris (1993: x):

> It is racism that has determined the manner in which their labour-power has been utilized; it is racism that has determined the manner in which their 'communities' have been policed; it is racism which assaults their humanity in psychiatric hospitals; and it is the effects of racism, too, that have been internalized. In short, it is racism against which the struggle has to be fought. Not difference.

When accounting for how national culture is entangled in UK marketing, I draw on writing about 'the difficulty of trying to *settle* the meaning of western multiculturalism within a national vortex of unsettled and unsettling diverse accounts of its implications, values and trajectories' (Hesse, 2000: ix). So, I turn to critical work on nationalism, marketing, and the commodification of race and cultural difference (Hesse, 2000; hooks, 1992; Johnson et al., 2019). The specificity of my focus on the UK enables analysis of how nationalism is implicated in brand responses to crises.

When using the term 'commodification', I do so to recognize actions and processes that involve treating something and / or someone as a mere commodity and / or a way to aid commercial activities. More than that, I use this term to acknowledge how concepts and experiences of care are embroiled in a racial capitalist system (Johnson, 2020)[1], and to comment on how this benefits certain institutions and, even, individuals, while harming other people. In writing about such forms of commodification I have remained wary of using this term as a mere 'shorthand to describe capitalism's co-option of potentially resistive subcultures' (Saha, 2012: 739). As Saha

---

[1] The vital writing of Dr Azeezat Johnson includes research and work on Black geographies, Black Muslim women's lives, Blackness in Britain, Black feminism, and anti-racist scholarship and knowledge production. This is by no means a complete account of all such brilliant work which has shaped and enriched the lives of so many people, and which continues to do so in ways that my words could never do justice to fully expressing. I encourage readers to learn more about, and from, Dr Azeezat Johnson's work, including by engaging with published writing that is cited and referenced throughout and far beyond this book.

(2012) critiques, in some scholarship on race and commodi-fication, 'references to commodification are cursory, on the way to another point, but at worst they represent a somewhat lethargic description of capitalism's supposed co-option of the counter-narratives of difference and the production of its own form of corporate multiculture' (739).

Instead of simply commenting on examples of co-option, my discussion of the commodification of care considers how institutions seek to construct, and, even, consume, or capture (Táíwò, 2022), care. Throughout my analysis, I think through how care is constructed and contorted, such as by reflecting on the problems of 'post-racial'[2] perspectives of 'universal care' which do not address how racism impacts experiences and expectations of care and comfort. I also acknowledge that UK marketing and public messaging that essentially encourages people to 'keep calm and consume' reflects a long history of consumption being framed as crucial to being a 'good' (British) citizen. A deep discussion of histories of colonialism and racism is beyond the scope of this brief book, but I of course recognize the ongoing impacts of both 'Euromodern colonialism' (Gordon, 2022: 13) and racism, including on the lives of Black and Asian people who are often structurally and interpersonally denied forms of care and comfort.

---

[2]The term 'post-racial' encompasses a point in time and/or part of society that is thought to exist in a way that is not impacted by issues concerning race and racism. My position aligns with what is outlined in the impactful work of communication scholar Professor Ralina L. Joseph, who uses the term 'postrace' as a way 'to name the ideology – sceptically – and to point out the continued centrality of race in this ideology where race is ostensibly immaterial' (Joseph, 2018: 8).

As writer and researcher Amelia Horgan (2021) argues in *Lost in Work: Escaping Capitalism*, '[t]he first stage of the crisis has shown that workers are exposed to very different levels of risk; some of us have been able to work from home, uncomfortable and difficult as that can sometimes be, while others have had no choice but to risk exposure to a potentially deadly virus' (2). 'Care' and 'normal' are words that frequently feature in public messaging that may be intended to mask inequalities that impact who tends to be cared for, who tends to do care work, and how temporary terms such as 'key worker' and 'essential worker' operate. However, when rooted in a disability justice framework, critical discussions of care (work) can contribute to efforts to address ableism and intersecting oppressions such as sexism, misogyny, homophobia, xenophobia, transphobia, classism, and racism. In the poignant words of poet, writer, educator, and social activist Leah Lakshmi Piepzna-Samarasinha (2018: 19):

> Everywhere people are talking about care work, emotional labour, femme emotional labor, access, and crip skills and science. None of this happened because the able-bodied people decided to be nice to the cripples. It happened because disabled queer and trans people of color started organizing, often with femme disabled Black and brown queer women in the lead.

The dynamic between marketing, rhetoric, and representations of care has been laid bare in work prior to this book (Chatzidakis and Littler, 2022; Chatzidakis, et al., 2020; Gonsalves and Kapcyznski, 2020; Kay and Wood, 2020; Littler, 2008; Sobande, 2020a, 2021a; Sobande and Klein, 2022; The Care Collective, 2020). Still, there is a need for more work that breaks down how racial capitalism, discourses of multiculturalism, and colonialist constructions of 'good citizenry' are implicated in experiences of, and allusions to, care and camaraderie during the COVID-19 crisis. There is also scope for more scrutiny of the entwined raced, gendered, and classed politics surrounding notions of 'normal life', care, comfort, and the time before COVID-19 – including by examining brand responses to the pandemic and interconnected crises such as structural anti-Blackness.

Consequently, this book is inspired by work that departs from whitewashed critiques of capitalism and which addresses the racist foundations of much of consumer culture and forms of care(lessness) (Crockett, 2021; hooks, 1992; Johnson et al., 2019). For these reasons, the analysis that follows is informed by philosopher and political thinker Lewis Gordon's (2022) account of the *Fear of Black Consciousness*, which discusses the destructive effects of neoliberalism, 'whose mantra is "privatization". Under that rubric, it valorizes abstract and moralistic notions of "the individual" as though each person is an individual god capable of determining the conditions of their needs by themselves' (11).

Additionally, Gordon (2022: 11) observes that '[t]he neo-conservative response to the crises of neoliberalism is to look back instead of forward'. I regard marketed nostalgia concerning perceptions of 'normal life' before COVID-19 as forming one of neoliberalism's many tentacles. It is not that I think all nostalgia for how life was experienced before this time is neoliberal in nature. Rather, I note that brands have capitalized on such nostalgia and experiences of longing, in ways that are consistent with neoliberalism's emphasis on participating in consumer culture to self-soothe. As well as drawing on Gordon's (2022) insightful work, this book is guided by extensive efforts to tackle unequal access to care and recognition of care work (Johnson, 2020; Piepzna-Samarasinha, 2018).

THE RHETORIC OF THE COVID-19 CRISIS

At the end of 2021, while eating chocolates wrapped in paper patterned with printed quotes, and when sitting with the heaviness of grieving my dad (a year after my nain), I came across these words attributed to tormented Dutch artist Vincent Van Gogh: 'Normality is a paved road: It's comfortable to walk but no flowers grow'. When reading that statement at the cusp of a new year marked by COVID-19's relentlessness, and while missing loved ones, I thought about the concept of comfort without flourishing, and normality without nurturing – what a world.

What is a world of comfort that is also a world without flowers? Who might find such a world comfortable and who might find it inhospitable? Also, how does media and marketing discourse depict and (de)politicize comfort in ways that are at odds with a caring world where both flowers *and* people grow? This book is rooted in such a preoccupation with the politics, power, and possibilities of care(lessness) and comfort, including consideration of the animating force of angst that society seeks to squash without addressing the structural issues that spark such feelings.

'New Normal', 'Levelling Up', and 'Eat Out to Help Out' are just a few of the expressions that encapsulate how the COVID-19 pandemic has been framed in UK press, politics, and public relations spheres. An indication of how ideas about normality have been linked to the crisis include a Collins Dictionary (2021) definition which alludes to the pandemic and a preoccupation with productivity. This explanation of 'normality' states that '[a] semblance of normality has returned with people going to work and shops re-opening'. As the emergence and spread of COVID-19 came to dominate much of mainstream media between 2020–2022, so too did messaging that made a nod to 'times before now', while speculating about the uncertain and assumed future, and overlooking that the UK's crisis of (a lack of) care predates the pandemic. To turn to the incisive words and work of Black (and) Muslim geographies scholar Azeezat Johnson (2020), 'part of what people are processing in this moment is that the same systems that have been failing *dis-eased* Others could now also fail them'.

Since March 2020, marketed slogans and soundbites intended to inspire people to 'come together' have surfaced at a similar rate to the COVID-19 virus itself – from well-meaning mantras that are meant to cultivate a call-to-action, to sycophantic branding activities that reflect the grasps of capitalism (Sobande, 2020a, 2021a; Sobande and Klein, 2022). As Chatzidakis et al. (2020: 890) aptly put it, there 'has thus been a discursive explosion of care across the global landscape'. I argue that such a discursive explosion of care dovetails with a discursive explosion regarding rhetoric related to so-called 'normal' life, in addition to discourse on, and derisions of, 'wokeness' (Kanai and Gill, 2021; Sobande et al., 2022), which are discussed further in Chapter 2. Such discourse(s) reflect dominant ideas about who and what is familiar and admirable, and who and what is weird and deviant, which connects to pervasive societal 'technologies of black subordination' (Gordon, 2022: 15).

With so many headlines and catchphrases in orbit of understandings of COVID-19, there is no shortage of words and brand approaches to reflect on when exploring the commodification of care and the coronavirus crisis, including the trite treatment of 'togetherness' in adverts. As Chatzidakis et al. (2020: 889) affirm, '[c]are, in all its permutations, is the buzzword of the moment, its meanings draining away in its constant evocation'. Therefore, although consideration of care is at the centre of this book, I also discuss associated feelings and ideas that are present in adverts that frame brands as caring (e.g., activism, inclusivity, loyalty, comfort, empowerment). While doing so, I acknowledge that austerity in the UK is implicated in this, and that such austerity and the intersecting inequalities that are part of it, form state-sponsored machinery which maintains oppressive and racial capitalist power relations (Bassel and Emejulu, 2018; Emejulu and Bassel, 2018). As extensive research on 'Minority women, austerity and activism' makes clear, '[a]part from being disproportionately affected by the cuts, minority women are also undermined by dominant discourses which can (mis)represent them as either "victims" or "enterprising actors"' (Emejulu and Bassel, 2015: 86). Also, as has been observed by Chatzidakis et al. (2020: 889):

> For decades so many have resolutely ignored ongoing environmental calamities, and the ever mounting refugee crisis, alongside the abject misery caused in this prolonged period of austerity capitalism, especially for those with significant caring responsibilities. Yet, suddenly, at least on the rhetorical level, we are seeing our governments being forced to put people before profits, however temporarily.

Attentive to such matters and informed by work on the cultural politics of emotion (Ahmed, 2004) and 'modes of activism within contemporary culture' (Mukherjee and Banet-Weiser, 2012: 1), I examine how a range of rhetorical devices and representations have been mobilized as part of marketplace responses to COVID-19 (e.g., discourses of patriotism, pride, and togetherness). In doing so, my work wrestles with notions of 'normality' and 'newness' – who and what determines the so-called 'new normal' and when it apparently commences?

My work engages with how oppressive ideas about a socially constructed and deviant 'Other' are shaped by the forms of stigmatization that sociologist Imogen Tyler (2020) conceptualizes as being 'a practice that, while experienced intimately through stigmatising looks, comments, slights, remarks made in face-to-face or digitally mediated encounters, is always enmeshed with wider capitalist structures of expropriation, domination, discipline and social control' (17). Relatedly, the vital work of writer, poet, educator, and activist Suhaiymah Manzoor-Khan (2022) in *Tangled in Terror: Uprooting Islamophobia* critically outlines 'A history of race-making: Inventing "the Muslim threat"', providing an in-depth account of systems of oppression at the centre of 'British values'. Overall, informed by such writing, and more, the crux of my book is a concern with how 'commodified notions of connection, care and community' have accelerated against the backdrop of COVID-19 (Sobande, 2020a, 2021a).

Building on extant work which examines 'desperate attempts by corporations to promote themselves as "caring"' (Chatzidakis et al., 2020: 889), while questioning the range of sometimes contradictory ways that care is defined in society, I consider dynamics between ideas regarding care, comfort, and normality – as are made manifest in the form of adverts that are intended to secure brands' longevity. Such analysis is informed by writing which critiques the societal 'logic of relegating care work to the unpaid realms of the personal' (Dowling, 2021: 3), which is a message that many brands promote to push their so-called 'self-care' products.

Like many, for me, 2020–2022 has involved the loss of loved ones – both family and friends in different spaces and places, including the context of a care home at the start of the pandemic. It has been, and still is, a time of immense grief and intense reflection regarding the reality of who society deems worthy of care and substantial forms of sustained comfort. As Gordon (2022: 11) notes in relation to North America, but which is also applicable to the UK, a noticeable 'decline in social services continues the production of vulnerability'. While many people were left to languish during the COVID-19 crisis, self-satisfied politicians and insecure brands strategically invoked sentimentality and sought to uphold an imagined unity by claiming that 'we're all in this together'. Yet, during that time, the cost of many things – from food and electricity to petrol and homes – has sharply risen and is likely to do so again.

The proliferation of political messaging about us all being 'in this together' coincided with a point in time when various Conservative MPs brazenly blocked plans to extend free school meals over the holiday period. The UK's last Labour government committed to end child poverty by 2020 (Streeting, 2021), but the Conservative party have been in government since 2010, and child poverty remains a significant issue – resulting in the creation of charities such as Zarach which delivers 'beds and basics to children in poverty' (www.zarach.org/).

Since I began writing this book, the UK's inflation rate hit a new 40-year high of 9.1% and the cost-of-living crisis went from bad to worse – leaving many (more) people destitute. During the final days of working on this chapter, the UK railway network's biggest strike in 30 years commenced, and, rightly, bolstered talk of the prospect of a general strike across sectors. This was all while the UK government was 'busy' attempting to defend their plans to send asylum seekers to Rwanda – plans that have been criticized by the European Court of Human Rights, and plans which, so far, have been disrupted by the essential activism and interventions of those committed to challenging xenophobia and the UK's hostile environment. Despite all of this, the government has continued to claim that they 'care', and to push messages of 'togetherness', while systematically stripping away the welfare state, and now, shambolically seeking to select a new Prime Minister following the scandalous actions of Boris Johnson.

Between moments of memorializing and attempting to make sense of the current condition(s) of the world, I found myself thinking about how togetherness was being (re)defined in ways that demand careful attention and critique. In Spring 2020 this led to me writing the following:

> [w]hile it is true that the impact of COVID-19 has affected the lives of many people around the world, not everyone is experiencing this crisis the same way, due to structural inequalities and intersecting oppressions. What is the relationship between COVID-19, capitalism and consumer culture? Who is the 'we' in the messages of 'we're all in this together', and how might such messages mask distinct socio-economic disparities and enable institutions to evade accountability? (Sobande, 2020a: 1033)

Just as ideas about who and what are 'normal' depend on ideas about who and what is not, marketing messages about who 'we' are, involve alluding to who 'we' are not, or, at least, who 'we' do not want to be. Accounting for this, I study adverts that simultaneously signal who is and who is not perceived to be part of the sense of togetherness that has been promoted and praised during the pandemic. This involves examining media and marketing material that (de)values different lives and activities through its promotion of entwined messages about consumer culture and social relations (e.g., 'Eat Out to Help Out').

Although I focus on the COVID-19 crisis, my analysis attends to continuities and contingencies concerning the themes of care, cultural citizenship, and branding, with attention particularly paid to how consumption features in this. My work is approached from a critical perspective which recognizes the necessary nature of people's scepticism of brands' actions and motives, such as by them scrutinizing 'greenwashing' (Littler, 2008; Miller, 2017), which involves challenging superficial brand attempts to portray themselves as environmentally friendly or as climate justice advocates.

Academia's individualistic culture of claiming to 'coin' certain terms means that scholars may be compelled to 'find' or use catch-all expressions such as 'brand activism' to describe some of the ways that brands are implicated in socio-political issues and appearing to take a stance on them. However, as I outline in this work, the term 'brand activism' may be little more than a repackaged oxymoron which is (strategically) used to imply that brands and their advocates are not self-interested.

It is telling that much marketing scholarship suggests that people's mistrust and / or scrutiny of brands is inherently negative and should be remedied. As discourses of 'brand activism' and 'corporate social initiatives (CSIs)' can foil or foist themselves on the coattails of structural change, I ruminate on the relationship between care, activism, and the COVID-19 crisis. Subsequently, I affirm that rejecting the notion of 'brand activism' opens up critical discussions of care and commodification in ways that move away from prioritizing the predatory perspectives and desires of brands. There are ways to differentiate between how brands comment on or claim to address societal issues, but that can be described without grasping at the label of 'activism' and without deifying brands or confusing consumerism for care. Unfortunately, discourses of 'brand activism' are sometimes (re)presented as being sociopolitically radical in nature, despite seeming to be little more than a way to advance towards careerist and commercial goals (e.g., becoming the authority on how to do *and* conceptualize 'brand activism' the 'right way'). As I go on to detail, the rise of earnest references to 'woke marketing' and how to effectively achieve it, is additional evidence of the expanding industry of commerce-oriented work that is positioned as aiding alleged 'activism' while ultimately assuaging the ego of brands. The language and logic of relatively dated terms, such as corporate social responsibility (CSR) and CSIs, alone, are insufficient tools with which to critically consider the commodification of care and the COVID-19 crisis. For this reason, although I draw on words and ideas that originate and are embraced within various business-related domains, my engagement with such concepts is critical and often entails questioning the assumptions that they are based on (e.g., whose and what definition of activism animates ideas about alleged 'brand activism'? whose and what definition of 'corporate social initiatives' is advocated as part of efforts to dismiss critique of brands?).

I draw on inspiration from a wide range of work, including writer and editor Leah Cowan's (2021) *Border Nation: A Story of Migration*, which critiques the violent and colonial power dynamics surrounding subjective and transient terms such as 'skilled worker'.

I am also spurred on by the scholarship of Moya Bailey and Izetta Autumn Mobley (2018: 34) on 'A Black feminist disability framework', which contends that '[a]ll too often people ask what is a respectable job, rather than offering a critique of a service economy or the globalizing socioeconomic system that demands more and more labor for less and less pay'. In addition to this, my work continues to be shaped by sociologist Ruha Benjamin's (2019) expansive explanation of transactional models of citizenship which frame the 'value' of citizens in ways pertaining to their potential spending power and market participation.

While writing this book I often (re)turned to the poignant writing of Azeezat Johnson (2020), who wrote of how 'COVID-19 and other coronaviruses have been treated as a problem of East Asia: so many of us bought into the belief that the borders informing the West would protect us from this plague and so we could divorce from the disaster of these diseases'. Accordingly, I consider contemporary concepts of what it means to be a so-called 'good citizen' in the UK, and how these ideas connect to capitalism, including racist, nationalistic, and xenophobic systems of value (Manzoor-Khan, 2022). As Gordon (2022: 12) articulates:

> The turn to xenophobia has its bedfellows in racism, misogyny, homophobia, and hatred of all those who are considered outsiders. The reactionary turn rejects the idea of countries such as Brazil, India, the United Kingdom, and the United States as citizens of the world and replaces it with nationalism premised on cherry-picked values from each country's past under the aegis of 'tradition.' Premised on anti-difference, this appeal expresses notions of purity.

Mindful of insights shared by both Johnson (2020) and Gordon (2022), the subsequent chapters pay attention to how notions of national / cultural identity and citizenship, as well as concepts of care, have moved around as part of media and marketing approaches during the coronavirus pandemic. 'Despite all the efforts of white power, SARS-CoV-2 (the novel coronavirus) doesn't "see" national borders, race, or any other boundary' (Gordon, 2022: 15). However, as I go on to discuss, some media and marketing professionals do see such distinctions, and even create content that upholds them.

RACIAL CAPITALISM AND CONSTRUCTIONS OF CARE AND COMFORT

As the ever-resonant work of Azeezat Johnson (2020) expresses with incomparable clarity, experiences of COVID-19 cannot be understood without taking seriously the ongoing impact of racial capitalism (Robinson, 1983), including its specific impact on the lives of Black disabled and chronically ill people. Critical considerations of care and its commodification must contend with power relations that underpin (in)access to both care and comfort (Ahmed, 2004), and must address the effects of racial capitalism which 'is the macro-structural context that helps shape the character of racial oppression in capitalist political economies' (Crockett, 2021: 3).

To be precise, as Johnson's (2020) writing has highlighted, exploitation within the structures and strictures of racial capitalism, including societal treatment of Black people as a mere means to commercial ends, impacts experiences of disability, chronic illness, and care(lessness). Taking heed of such matters, 'disability justice means a political movement and many interlocking communities where disability is not defined in white terms, or male terms, or straight terms ... Disability justice centers sick and disabled people of colour, queer and trans disabled folks of color, and everyone who is marginalized in mainstream disability organizing' (Piepzna-Samarasinha, 2018: 22).

What is the relationship between societal concepts and experiences of care and social justice? Who and what is depicting care during the COVID-19 crisis in the UK, and with what effects? I 'finished' this book more than two years on from first scribbling some initial thoughts on the dynamics between care, commodification, and COVID-19. Since then, the number of advertising campaigns and mission statements by brands claiming to care has mushroomed. In turn, so too has writing about the ways that brands try to stay relevant, while weathering the storm of this crisis and the infinite others that it connects to (e.g., anti-Blackness and the cost-of-living crisis in the UK). Although there is now more writing regarding how market logics mediate messaging and decisions surrounding COVID-19, there is scarce consideration of the connections between the cultural politics of emotion (Ahmed, 2004), nation(alistic) branding (Aronczyk, 2013), and the current crisis.

Even within the widening world of critiques of rampant consumerism during the COVID-19 pandemic, there is often a lack of recognition of the role of racial capitalism and white supremacy in this, including how the societal treatment of Black people as commodities throughout history, has contoured components of current commercial and care(less) conditions. 'The preexisting pandemics of neoliberalism, neoconservatism, fascism, and their accompanying racism created social sites of vulnerability' (Gordon, 2022: 15) which enabled the spread of coronavirus in many countries, such as the UK. As well as attending to aspects of the history of this place, my book reflects on complex components of comfort – including why comfort often appears to be an afterthought amid scholarly and societal conversations concerning care.

Who gets to be / feel comfortable?

Who does society permit to pursue comfort?

How do (dis)comfort and precarity (dis)connect?

I parse the push and pull of structural power and individual (as well as collective) agency, to grasp how the relationship between them configures care, comfort, and their commodification. Informed by work which argues that 'we are in need of a politics that recognises our mutual interdependence and vulnerability' (Chatzidakis et al., 2020), I affirm that such politics has long been a part of the work of Black and distability activists, and I make the case for considering how powerful expressions of angst and boundary-work are enmeshed in such matters. This involves thinking about 'questions of inequality and power in Britain and beyond' (Hesse, 2000: iix), which 'are constitutive of the western formations in which cultural differences, particularly structured around race, ethnicity and gender, are *recurrently politicized*' (ibid.).

At the heart of my book is a call for comfort to be as equally prioritized as care, but without this occurring in ways that fuel consumer culture or which prop up practices predicated on the exploitation of others. In outlining this, I think through different meanings and modes of comfort, particularly those that entail sitting with both grief and hope. 'Thought draws the imaginary of the past: a knowledge becoming' (Glissant, 1997) to help realize the potential of the future and forms of both care and comfort that it may hold. With this in mind, the possibilities of acknowledging and acting in response to angst are discussed in the pages that follow, with a focus on its crucial role in critiquing the carelessness of institutions.

WHERE NEXT?

It is on-brand for brands to pursue profit, such as by using superficial marketing gestures propelled by pomp, pride, posturing, and a penchant for adverts that allude to activism without committing to it. So, it is unsurprising that brands have sought to make money during this time, including by crassly invoking care and community. Elements of my prior and collaborative work highlight that many brands appear to prioritize profit over people (Rosa-Salas and Sobande, 2022; Sobande and Klein, 2022) – something that I am far from being the first person to point out. But what is of more interest to me here is *how* brands have sought to convey that they care during this crisis, *who* and *what* they have claimed to care about, as well as *why* various critiques of branding activity present the politic(ization) of brands as something 'new' and stop short of skewering capitalism.

The work of Chatzidakis et al. (2020: 89) on 'carewashing' illuminates examples of how brands attempt to convey that they care about people and particular societal issues. In dialogue with wider work on care and consumer culture, such research by Chatzidakis et al. (2020) elucidates that 'underlining these representations and proclamations are often disturbing assumptions about what counts as meaningful care'. Influenced by such work, my book includes analysis of adverts to consider how brands attempt to construct and convey (that they) care, as well as examination of institutions' approaches to corporate communications in the form of social media strategies.

Chapter 2 dissects discourse that enables the pretense of alleged 'brand activism' – ranging from the façade of fast fashion to the marketization of university life. As I delineate, claims of 'brand activism' and efforts to guard the image of those who advocate for CSIs reveal much about the world of branding, academia, and their shared investment in capitalist market logics (Rosa-Salas and Sobande, 2022). Chapter 2 reflects on why scholarship on 'brand activism' often upholds the assumption that brands can be activists, and in ways that (re)define activism to appease brands and their stakeholders. There, I also consider why scholarly writing on supposed 'brand activism' and CSIs offers brands ways to gain 'consumer trust' and maintain their image – a proposition that clashes with the principles of much grassroots activism – namely, anti-capitalist movements.

The penultimate part of Chapter 2 critiques some of the ways universities have attempted to comment on International Women's Day (IWD) and Black Lives Matter (BLM), including by issuing statements about the latter to 'show that the values of the university do not support racism. Some directly referred to "Black Lives Matter", some referred to racism, others spoke about BAME[3] communities and some referred to diversity generally' (Halpin, 2020: 8). The final part of Chapter 2 examines how an advert by British banking brand Halifax demonstrates one of the ways that care and consumerism appear to be conflated in marketing during times of crisis.

Chapter 3's smorgasbord includes analysis of cleaning supplies, disinfectant, and antiseptic company Dettol's 'back to work' campaign, which appeared at a point when lockdown measures were starting to ease. Subsequently, I focus on memory-making during crises and forms of grieving

---

[3]'BAME' is an acronym for 'Black, Asian and minority ethnic' – a categorizing term that is commonly used in the UK and which is much contested due to the potential for it to diminish distinct differences between the lives of people from a range of racial and ethnic backgrounds.

(both intimately and aloud), by considering how connections between consumer culture and (the mirage of) memories can colour experiences of nostalgia, reminiscing, and grief. Then, I critically examine the government's framing of the UK's 'Eat Out to Help Out' discount scheme and consider how influencer culture has (and has not) altered during the COVID-19 crisis.

Chapter 3 wraps up with a consideration of what the rise (pun intended!) of banana bread and its online documentation during the crisis suggests about elements of the racial, gender, and class politics of notions and experiences of productivity and rest. I reflect on how discourse that surrounded home-baking and its Instagrammable aestheticization during the pandemic may ultimately uphold middle-class notions of domesticity in ways that simultaneously mask the labour of baking and obfuscate the predominantly precarious and working-class labour of those who farm and provide the ingredients that make such baking possible. In thinking this through, I critically account for moments when home-baking during the crisis was misguidedly equated with a radical refusal to bend to societal pressures of productivity by appearing to embrace seemingly 'restful', yet often essentially gendered and 'traditional'[4] practices of home life.

---

[4] I would like to thank Professor of Sociology, Akwugo Emejulu, for a generative question on the potential relationship between the social media documentation/framing of home-baking and the ascent of digital discourse that promotes the conservative and heteronormative values of 'tradwives'. This question was asked during the final days of completing the finishing touches of this book, and in response to my presentation on '"Watch me work": Discourses of productivity, precarity, presenteeism, and the pandemic' which I delivered online as part of a hybrid format symposium on 'Freelance Feminism' (City, University of London, 22 June, 2022), organized by Hannah Curran-Troop, Professor Rosalind Gill, and Professor Jo Littler.

Finally, as I feel my shoulders begin to drop, and the speed of my thoughts soothingly slow down, Chapter 4 looks to the future in a way that involves returning to some of the key questions and points posed earlier in the book. I speculate about the world that may lie ahead, while holding onto the hope that endures.

When the words 'normal' were / are uttered during the COVID-19 crisis, whose experiences were / are being prioritized, and how? When people were encouraged to 'Eat Out to Help Out', what did such a message suggest about the connection between consumer culture and the concept of being a 'good (British) citizen'? Overall, this book is bolstered by such considerations and a commitment to critiquing the commodification of care and crises, while calling for a world where neither comfort nor care is a luxury reserved for a select few.

2

BEYOND THE PRETENSE OF 'BRAND ACTIVISM'

The world of advertising has been depicted in many different pop culture contexts, but the critically acclaimed televised drama series *Mad Men* (2007–2015) stands out from the crowd. Among the show's iconic season finales is The Wheel (episode 13 of season 1, 2007), which captures the power of advertising. The show's main protagonist Don Draper (played by Jon Hamm) finds himself delivering an impactful client pitch to Kodak. This involves Don reflecting on how consumer culture – namely, products and their advertising – can stir people's emotions and speak to their souls.

In earnest, and to an initially stiff client audience, Don speaks of how 'technology is a glittering lure, but there is the rare occasion when the public can be engaged on a level beyond flash, if they have a sentimental bond with the product'. Don goes on to discuss 'nostalgia', including its delicate yet potent nature. By turning to sentimentality, he demonstrates his ability to highlight how Kodak's product movingly brings photographs to life. In turn, Don proves his potential to help Kodak successfully market The Wheel (which he affectionately refers to as The Carousel).

Brands consist of people, practices, and promises that play a part in the pursuit of a profitable profile and platform – including by stirring emotions and trying to conjure nostalgia. From the celebrities and logos associated with household supermarket names, to the social media handles and partnerships of influencers – a brand's image is made up of different texts, signs, and symbols. In some situations, 'brand' is deemed to be a dirty word that connotes the cravings and cruelties of capitalism. In other settings, the term 'brand' invokes prestige and a praised power to influence. In almost all circumstances, 'brand' is an expression that conjures up images and ideas of commercial activity and marketplace exchanges, including shopping transactions. But not all brands want to be associated with consumerism, and some even put a lot of effort into attempting to camouflage the market logic and exploitation that lies beneath their polished surface.

This chapter examines the marketing of brands who have claimed to care, convey a sense of comfort, and / or constructed camaraderie during the COVID-19 crisis (e.g., Boohoo, Deliveroo, Halifax). Such analysis investigates how the themes of normality, heroism, patriotism, and togetherness are drawn on by brands to promote their products and services in ways that allude to constructions of care and comfort (Sobande and Klein, 2022). In addition to considering such matters, I scrutinize an aspect of the public sector – UK higher education – that has sought to both distance itself from, and embrace, branding practices. The subsequent discussion reiterates the reality that brands have been political and politicized for much longer than is sometimes suggested by claims that '[b]rands are now seemingly comfortable alienating some consumers to address contested and polarizing sociopolitical issues' (Vredenburg et al., 2020: 445).

This chapter also clarifies contradictions and contortions inherent to how the term 'woke-washing' – which relates to marketing approaches – has been used in scholarly and marketing industry settings. I critique how such a term has been taken up in ways that move away from critically examining brands, their harmful actions, and their hypocrisy, to move towards helping them disguise their actions and / or manage backlash. As I reflected on for *Disegno*:

> For more than five years [now, seven], as part of my research into the media experiences of Black women in Britain, I have been exploring how brands attempt to portray themselves as supporters of Black and social justice activism. The assumed woke attributes of brands have been praised by some media, but this form of strategic marketing can symbolically, and sometimes ambiguously, merely gesture towards activism. A case in point is when brands are celebrated for featuring images of activists in their campaigns, regardless of the reality that many companies' dubious employment conditions are at odds with the principles of racial justice upheld by the activists that they aspire to be associated with. (Sobande, 2020c)

Before examining how brands have presented themselves as caring, while also reflecting on hues of higher education that hint at its unrepentant marketization, I pause to consider the politics of care, (dis)comfort, and commodification. This means engaging with a range of work on care and capitalism, which I now turn to (Bailey and Mobley, 2018; Chatzidakis and Littler, 2022; Chatzidakis et al., 2020; Gonsalves and Kapcyznski, 2020; Johnson, 2020; Piepzna-Samarasinha, 2018; The Care Collective, 2021).

THE POLITICS OF CARE(LESSNESS), (DIS)COMFORT, AND COMMODIFICATION

When I think of care, I think of unwavering and collective forms of support that are essential to survival but are about much more than stoicism or ableist notions of strength. I think of both the tenderness of love offered and reciprocated, and the sharpness of healthcare systems where medical racism and xenophobia remains rife. I think of the contradictions present in contexts that are claimed as sites of care but that are also spaces where care-lessness runs rampant. Experiences of care, of course, involve many forms of essential clinical work, as is palpably present during the ongoing coronavirus pandemic. However, if care is conceptualized in purely clinical terms, there is a risk that care is constructed and delivered in ways that do not account for people's desire and need for care that places comfort (emotionally, physically, spiritually, and psychically) at its core. What is care without agency, comfort, gentleness, and grace? Is it care at all?

Arguably, the coronavirus pandemic 'has finally foregrounded "care" as a keyword of our time – one that hitherto had remained largely peripheral in the lexicon of the left, despite the persistent efforts of a long line of feminist theorists' (Chatzidakis et al., 2020: 890), particularly those involved in disability justice work. However, the word comfort is often still glaringly absent from many mainstream conversations concerning care, as is consideration of how addressing the (dis)comfort of some people is societally prioritized (e.g., middle-class people) in comparison to addressing the (dis)comfort of others (e.g., working-class people).

In other words, discourse on care is sometimes steeped in expectations of unwavering stoicism and resilience – which is expected of both carers and those who they care for, and which does not account for how structural forms of oppression impact who tends to experience specific vulnerabilities, harms, and the material conditions to access care (and comfort). 'Care, like all other human practices and emotions, always fluctuates, and is frequently at odds with other needs and affective states, such as the desire for personal gratification and recognition' (Chatzidakis et al., 2020: 890). In the context of neoliberalism, care and comfort are commonly constructed and understood in ways that are tethered to market logics and even expectations of customer service. Expressions such as 'service with a smile' and 'bedside manner' feature as part of media, political, and public discussions of experiences of care, including praise or critique of the extent to which a care-worker is deemed to be personable, friendly, and attentive.

I echo calls for forms of comfort to more effectively be provided alongside care, while recognizing that '[t]he availability of comfort for some bodies may depend on the labour of others' (Ahmed, 2004: 149). Expectations of comfort and care (e.g., who provides them, and how) are raced, gendered, and classed in ways which yield distinctly different expectations and societal treatment of care-workers, such as those faced by a Black working-class woman who is a nurse, compared to those experienced by a white middle-class man who is a doctor. Hence, when calling for forms of comfort to be more firmly embedded in experiences of care, it is important to recognize how the different pressures and problems faced by care-workers are impacted by racism, sexism, misogyny, classism, and their many intersections. This also means that pursuit of more meaningful forms of both comfort and care must include the comfort and care of carers, as well as those who they care for and about.

What would it mean to turn more attention to collectively ensuring that comfort is at the core of care, and to disentangling the way that consumer culture has sought to capture and capitalize on care and comfort? The purchase of various products – from food to clothes – can undoubtedly contribute to experiences of comfort and care. Yet, in some cases, consumer culture – including the purchase of products marketed as so-called 'self-care' essentials – may have the effect of making (some) people *feel* better, rather than resulting in them being so. As sociologist Bev Skeggs (2022) puts it as part of a recorded conversation with Rosie Hancock and Alexis Hieu Truong about care and its privatization, '[w]e're talking about something old that's been really, really commoditised. And absolutely, as you say, become a huge industry, and has also, by becoming so commodified, has eclipsed all sorts of different forms of care. It's almost as if it's eclipsed the interdependence of care that every form of care really relies on. So, it's impossible just to be self-caring'.

Relatedly, '[a] clear example of how feminist ideas have been decontextualised and recontextualised via consumer culture is the co-optation of Black lesbian feminist [Audre] Lorde's (1988) notion of "self-care" and its radical potential. Lorde's (1988) political position, which is undergirded by critiques of capitalism and its racist nature, is often reduced to marketing messages which insinuate that self-care exclusively starts and ends with consumerism' (Sobande, 2020b: 2725). Shaped by work such as that of Lorde's (1988), my critique of the commodification of care is not a critique of the fact that people pursue forms of care and comfort in their lives. Instead, I critique how consumer culture and its advocates seek to capture and redefine care and comfort, in ways that elide the reality of how commodification processes are part of the capitalist problems that prohibit many people's experiences of care and comfort.

Sure, at times, the purchase of a product or participation in the marketplace can play a part in how people experience a sense of comfort and pleasure, and I don't pretend to be above such purchasing habits. However, the aspirational joy, gentleness, and so-called 'soft life' that many brands (including influencers) claim to embody, should not be mistaken for the type of care that Lorde wrote of. Nor should the nature of care that Lorde (1988) outlined be assumed to be completely joyless and devoid of pleasure.

As the language of care and pleasure continues to be wrapped up in the promotion of products and the brands behind them, there is a need to stay alert to how classism and respectability politics is implicated in marketed notions of joy and rest. This includes some framings of Black joy which can be part of the depoliticizing efforts of market entities which construct happiness as a (purchasable) choice – one which is sometimes made possible by the discomfort and exploitation of other people, including those who are Black and are expected to take on many different types of low-paid, unpaid, and forced care work.

It is true that '[h]istorically, many forms of care and care work have been strongly associated with the "feminine"' (Chitzadakis et al., 2020: 890). As well as noting the gendered dimensions of care and care work, it is essential to account for their raced dimensions and how the two (gender *and* race) intersect (Bailey and Mobley, 2018; Johnson, 2020).

As Chatzidakis et al. (2020: 889) assert, 'the COVID-19 crisis is becoming firmly established as above all a *crisis of care'*, but whose experiences and perceptions of care (as well as comfort) tend to be prioritized during this time and are regarded as 'normal'? Johnson's (2020) writing reminds readers that, contrary to public messaging, care is not something afforded to all. This point is mirrored by the work of Gordon (2022: 10) who states that '[e]ven where black people may have equal access, it doesn't follow that there is no racism in the administering of medical services to us'.

The crisis of care(lessness) (Dowling, 2021) that has been experienced in recent years is the outcome of much more than the impact of the coronavirus pandemic. In the words of The Care Collective (2020: 1-2):

> long before the pandemic, care services had already been slashed and priced out of reach for many of the elderly and disabled, hospitals were routinely overwhelmed and in crisis, homelessness had been on the rise for years, and increasing numbers of schools had begun dealing with pupil hunger. Meanwhile, multinational corporations had been making huge profits out of financializing and overleveraging care homes while work in the care sector was subsumed into the corporate gig economy, making precarious workers not only more numerous but also hugely overstretched.

Care should involve individuals being treated with dignity and respect, while being cared for – whether that is an adult's experience of receiving medical treatment or a child's experience of different types of carers. As such, care-related activism includes the collective efforts of care experienced people such as those involved in Who Cares? Scotland (2022), who work 'to influence change which directly redresses the inequality that care experienced people face at both a community and national level'.

As Horgan (2021: 3) affirms, '[i]n a society that is highly unequal, like the UK, the conditions under which people will experience the same health problem will be vastly different. These differences are not secondary; rather they can define the likelihood of becoming sick and the severity of the illness itself'. Receiving care – whether as a baby, child, or adult – is not simply a matter of getting to access certain systems and services, such as the NHS. For example, research highlights that crucial healthcare equipment, such as oxygen meters (oximeters), work less well on dark skin than light skin, which means that the accuracy of readings for dark-skinned people can be considerably compromised (Feiner et al., 2007; Lovett, 2021). This is just one from a long list of issues which elucidate the harmful nature of 'post-racial' perspectives of 'universal care' which do not address issues regarding race, racism, colourism, and provision / experiences of care. Also, in the striking words of Skeggs (2022) on care and the NHS, 'until we come to face it, we don't actually know in the UK how much has been privatised. For instance, there's seven areas in the UK that have absolutely no social care support for the elderly. You can't get provision; you can't it's not there'. The privatization of health and social care existed before the COVID-19 pandemic but has undoubtedly played a part in the cruelty of the crisis.

The (mis)treatment that people do or do not receive, once they are within care systems, or when accessing related services, determines whether what they are receiving is care or is in fact the antithesis of it. Such experiences are always informed by the politics and history of the UK, where entrenched racism and xenophobia means that many Black and Asian people who work in care-based roles face abuse and discrimination while trying to do their (often low-paid) jobs.

To (re)turn to the clarion call of Johnson (2020):

> Even though People of Colour have repeatedly warned against the violence of the UK's nostalgia for empire, many took every opportunity to tell us that things weren't 'that bad': they argued that if only we were a bit more patient, if only we worked a bit harder, things would eventually get better.

As Johnson (2020) emphasizes, despite others' claims that the crisis of Brexit and COVID-19 have exposed issues of inequality, people who are structurally marginalized – including those who are Black and disabled – have actively acknowledged and challenged such inequalities long before then. The incisive words of Johnson (2020) echo elements of Bailey and Mobley's (2018: 20) crucial 'Black feminist disability framework', which 'centers race, gender, and disability, challenging these generally siloed theories to work together to better understand the realities for those multiply marginalized within society'.

The impacts of ableism, austerity, and the underfunding and understaffing of health and social care in the UK and elsewhere have never been hidden. Rather, they are often only meaningfully and societally acknowledged as issues once they significantly impact the lives of white and middle-class people on a large scale – such as in the form of a global pandemic. Despite how Brexit and the COVID-19 crisis are often referred to as having 'revealed' issues of inequality, such deep-seated issues are not new. Instead, they were, and still are, often ignored and denied by institutions and individuals who believe they are immune to their negative impacts.

When reflecting on the crisis of care(lessness) in the UK, and the structural oppression that Johnson (2020) names, I recalled the resonant words and wisdom of creative and restorative practitioner, cultural worker, and scholar Naya Jones (2021a) – whose work lifts up 'Black community health, healing, and ecologies, especially in the context of spatial injustice like gentrification or climate injustice'. Jones' (2021b) approach to 'black dream geographies' foregrounds the need to care for, and about, 'Black interiority' – whether that be Black people's experiences of dreaming while sleeping or dreaming while awake.

Informed by the generous work of both Johnson (2020) and Jones (2021a, 2021b, 2022), my critique of the commodification of care and the absence of comfort in various so-called care systems, acknowledges the experiences of individuals who others may perceive as receiving care, but who are not tended to in any meaningful, comforting, respectful, or care-full ways.

Writer, poet, philosopher, and literary critic Édouard Glissant's (1997) critical work on *Poetics of Relation* is integral to how I think through the differences between being cared for / about, and being (mis)treated, as well as the differences between being visually represented and being structurally supported. 'Action is not always about creating or doing something that is visible to others' (Sobande and Emejulu, 2021: 2), and so, care must be understood in ways that surpass a focus on what is visible or legible to all.

As Glissant's (1997) writing illuminates, it is important to move beyond the ineffective binary opposition of 'visible' and 'invisible', including to grasp how forms of recognition, retreat, resonance, refuge, and consequently, care, function and feel in society. Glissant's (1997: 189) call for 'the right to opacity' pushes against assumptions that all people want to be represented and recognized in the same way. Such work challenges the notion that forms of societal visibility and representation are inherently beneficial to the people who appear to be represented and recognized. So too does the insightful work of writer, scholar, and social activist bell hooks (1992) on *Black Looks: Race and Representation*, which critiques how 'marginalized groups, deemed Other, who have been ignored, rendered invisible, can be seduced by the emphasis on Otherness, by its commodification, because it offers the promise of recognition and reconciliation' (26).

Buoyed by the work of hooks (1992) and Glissant (1997), I engage with depictions and discourses of care, while respecting the intimacy, privacy, and, overall, *opacity*, of certain experiences of care (and experiences of a lack of it). Guided by such critical perspectives of visibility, opacity, and power, when reflecting on the relationship between activism and consumer culture, I acknowledge that '[i]deas regarding "real activism", can involve expectations of activism being very public and physical in nature, such as a protest march, or a demonstration "die-in"' (Sobande, 2018a: 84), and that, '[m]easuring the success of activism solely in relation to its visibility and the immediacy of its effects, can uphold neoliberal notions of productivity and speed over sustainability, that such activism may even be intended to resist' (ibid.).

Therefore, in writing this book, I recognize that much activism, including disability justice work, is 'underdocumented, private work – work often seen as not "real activism"' (Piepzna-Samarasinha, 2018: 19), despite its impact and importance. This means that, in principle, I agree with the sentiments of Gordon's (2022: 17) statement that '[t]he guiding theme of these pandemics – antidemocracy, colonialism, racism, and a disease – is invisibility', but the way that forms of visibility (e.g., marketing representations) and opacity (e.g., efforts to maintain intimacy and privacy) operate amid these pandemics requires further consideration. Then again, particularly when accounting for the ongoing 'state suppression of community organising' (Campbell, 2021) and the UK government's efforts to prohibit protests, it is important to acknowledge the power of direct action that takes necessary public forms.

The following section continues this conversation about visibility, representation, commodification, and care. I provide an overview of how such issues appear in the form of expressions and analysis of brand 'woke-washing' and 'woke capitalism' (Dowell and Jackson, 2020; Kanai and Gill, 2020; Orgad and Gill, 2022; Rhodes, 2021; Rossi and Táíwò, 2020; Sobande, 2020b; Vredenburg et al., 2020), 'feminist advertising' ('femvertising') (Banet-Weiser, 2018; Mukherjee and Banet-Weiser, 2012; Sobande, 2019), and, more recently, 'carewashing' (Chatzidakis and Littler, 2022; Chatzidakis et al., 2020). Focusing on key marketing examples, and how literature on 'woke-washing' and 'carewashing' has developed, I critique how different concepts of care, injustice, activism, and inequality are made manifest in marketing and related theorizations.

THE CONTRADICTIONS AND CONTORTIONS OF 'WOKE-WASHING' AND 'FEMVERTISING'

Understandings and ideas about 'wokeness' predate the twenty-first century. Such understandings and ideas include Black American novelist and writer William Melvin Kelley's (1962) notable, and now often cited, *The New York Times* article, 'If you're woke you dig it'. Yet, it is also vital to recognize key recent cultural moments that have influenced the direction of contemporary discourses of 'wokeness'. Jordan Peele's iconic film *Get Out* (2017) is one of many sources of such impact.

Get Out depicts the horrors of anti-Blackness and white supremacy, with a soundtrack that features Childish Gambino's song Redbone which includes lyrics about staying 'woke'. The laidback track plays during the opening of the film – its lyrics foreshadowing the horrors that lie ahead for the main protagonist, a young Black man named Chris Washington (played by Daniel Kaluuya), who hauntingly finds that he must stay alert (or, 'woke') to the nefarious intentions of his white girlfriend and her family. *Get Out* played a part in ushering in a wave of media and cultural commentaries on what it means to 'stay woke' – actively conscious of anti-Blackness and social injustices and invested in tackling such forms of violence and structural oppression.

Due to the 'diversity-capitalism nexus' (Rossi and Táíwò, 2020), 'contemporary consumer culture frequently employs the term "woke" in ways that whitewash its genesis, confusing capitalist endeavours and corporate spin with collective racial justice action and sustained organising' (Sobande, 2020c). The word 'woke' packs a political punch that has been contorted by craven individuals who are intent on weaponizing notions of 'wokeness' to undermine perspectives that contrast with their own. There is much evidence of people invoking ideas about 'wokeness' (Kanai and Gill, 2020), including when seeking to critique, and even, obstruct, the words of others who they argue are impeding 'free speech'. Put simply, the word 'woke' is often unironically flung around during discussions of 'free speech', including by proponents of 'free speech' who appear intent on preventing the so-called 'woke' from speaking freely. By extension, the term 'woke-washing' can be uttered in ways that are indicative of hypocrisy and some people's disdain for critiques of racial capitalism.

Debating the details of free speech is beyond the aims of this book, but it is necessary to understand how the word 'woke' functions in contradictory ways in different contexts, to grapple with the term 'woke-washing' and analysis of related marketplace activity during the COVID-19 crisis. While my use of this term ('woke-washing') has changed in the years since I began to write about it, what has remained relatively consistent is my cynicism regarding the potential for brands to be activists – unsurprisingly, I don't think they can.

More recently, I have also scrutinized different scholarly contortions of 'woke-washing' which appear to be embedded in an intention to defend brands, while establishing individuals' expertise in 'woke marketing' or while claiming to 'guard' against criticism of CSIs and business ethicists. Such scholarly accounts that I have examined include those that reprimand critics of brands and capitalism by dismissively invoking ideas such as 'moral purity' and 'moral perfectionism' (Warren, 2022), and without interrogating how such terms and their use are impacted by power relations regarding race, gender, and class.

'Woke-washing' is an expression which has been wielded and critiqued to (re)present scholarly ideas as 'new' and 'novel', when sometimes, perhaps they are merely a re-hash and dilution of (often uncredited, and Black) liberationist perspectives from days gone by. No matter how many proponents of 'woke marketing' or business ethics defensively dismiss critiques of brands who claim to care, society does not need a corporate saviour. However, corporations do need ways to resuscitate, rehabilitate, and rebrand their image, and strategically alluding to activism or framing themselves as an ally is one way to do so.

Those who try to crush critique of such brand activity often draw on a spectrum of scaremongering tactics, including by implying that terms such as 'woke-washing' disincentivize brands to 'do good'. The notion that people must avoid critiquing brands in order for brands to take seriously social injustice and inequalities reflects the power of capitalism and expectations that people submit to it.

By focusing on criticism of brands and not the structures that they are part of, those who claim that 'woke-washing' is nothing but a derogatory descriptor, ensure that critical discussion of macro issues (e.g., racial capitalism and white supremacy) is obfuscated. In some cases, such writing which dismisses critiques of brands and capitalism, upholds notions of 'wokeness' that uncritically stem from an understanding of the term that is tethered to its [white] mainstream appropriation as an expression of disdain that is used to disapprove of something and / or someone. The charges made against critics of brands, and their use of the term 'woke-washing', often reveal much about how racial capitalism guards itself – whether that be via the defensive actions of brands or the words of scholars who seem to believe that brands need saving.

When thinking through these matters, I have queried the function of questions regarding the attitudes and actions of brands, such as 'are inconsistences morally problematic?' (Warren, 2022: 183). This is but one of many questions that may initially seem anodyne, but I contend that the ambiguity of 'problematic' does a lot of heavy-lifting in this context. Who gets to authoratively determine what is (and is not) 'morally problematic' and how so-called 'moral purity' functions, is worthy of critical analysis.

Depending on who utters them, and exactly what they are referring to, statements laced with moral panic such as '[b]oth woke and woke washing critics are using labels to create stigmas that they hope will punish targeted firms through divestments, boycotts, or legislation when they engage in social issues' (Warren, 2022: 187) are sometimes little more than proxies for telling marginalized folk to know their place and quit calling out brands (and Big Business). For these reasons, I remain very wary of work that is quick to dismiss critiques of brands as nothing other than supposed 'moral purity' and 'moral perfectionism'.

More than that, some efforts to undermine critique of brands and capitalism draw on theories of philosophy that, at 'best', don't address race, and at worst, have promoted racist perspectives. As a result, I am reminded of how oppressive notions of morality that treat whiteness as their compass, have been rehashed for centuries in ways that oppress Black and other racialized people. Sometimes, I feel that much of the scholarship that debates and discusses the meanings and uses of terms such as 'woke-washing' is merely a distraction from the real issues at stake. Perhaps much of such work, conveniently, by continuing to toil over the trials and tribulations of terminology, enables individuals and institutions to avoid attempting to address the structural issues and inequalities that such terminology can be used in relation to.

When reading through accounts that scold people for critiquing brands, and which imply that 'woke-washing' is merely a derogatory term, I grimaced at the prospect of brands becoming a protected characteristic under the UK's fragile Equality Act – a law intended to prohibit discrimination. After the impact of a global pandemic that has destroyed lives and been entangled with racial capitalism, it speaks volumes that some spheres of academic and political life are focusing on admonishing individuals who deem the actions of brands and businesses to be harmful and / or hypocritical, rather than them tending to the structural stigmatization and oppression of people.

As the expansion of writing on the topics of 'woke-washing' and 'brand activism' illuminates, despite the term being one with the capacity to be used to critique brands and their claims to care, 'woke-washing' has also been taken up by marketers and scholars who seem committed to sustaining and aiding marketing practices by positing that brands should pursue a 'woke' image in an allegedly 'authentic' way.

Despite the rising number of accounts of 'brand activism', it is still my opinion that 'brands are often a component of the very structural problems that community organisers strive towards dismantling as part of liberationist work' (Sobande, 2021a). A case in point is that '[t]he imagined "we" that brands brazenly construct via adverts that are meant to tug on the heart strings of individuals during the pandemic is a "we" with money to spend. Such a "we" consists of consumption, not care, and profit, not people' (ibid). Such a 'we' *consumes* the crisis, rather than working collectively to address its harmful impacts and the inequalities that preceded it.

Differences between people's take on the topic of 'brand activism' may be, at least partly, due to what Hall (1997a, 1997b) described as being 'shared conceptual maps'. What I mean is that some people share a conceptualization of 'brand activism' which is based on a particular perspective of what constitutes both brands and activism, but which contrasts with the perspectives of other people who identify brands, by nature, as operating in ways that are at odds with activism. Such different opinions are evidence of how the discursive terrain of activism (e.g., how activism is (re)defined) is a site of struggle which involves various claims being staked – including in support of, or against, capitalism.

On that note, while there is a multitude of explanations of what the term 'woke-washing' is intended to encompass, to me, the expression can capture how and why 'approaches to feminism and Black activism [among other social justice movements] are drawn on in marketing content related to the concept of being "woke" (invested in addressing social injustices)' (Sobande, 2020b: 2723). 'Woke-washing' has been used in reference to how 'brands (mis)use issues concerning commercialised notions of feminism, equality and Black social justice activism as part of marketing that flattens and reframes liberationist politics while upholding the neoliberal idea that achievement and social change requires individual ambition and consumption rather than structural shifts and resistance' (ibid.). Relatedly, as Gordon (2022: 13) affirms, '[n]eoliberalism thus nurtures racism by undermining the conditions of addressing it. It is, in short, reckless', and brands capitalize on this by presenting people with the illusionary opportunity to overcome adversity through their consumption choices and brand loyalty (Rosa-Salas and Sobande, 2022).

As is considered in the work of scholars Enzo Rossi and Olúfẹmi O. Táíwò, (2020), although the term 'woke-washing' is a relatively recent one, the critiques of capitalism that the term sometimes supports has a long and multivocal history. This includes the legacy of the work of hooks (1992), who in the early 1990s wrote about how 'the commodification of difference promotes paradigms of consumption wherein whatever difference the Other inhabits is eradicated, *via* exchange, by a consumer cannibalism that not only displaces the Other but denies the significance of that Other's history through a process of decontextualization' (31).

In 2018, at the point that I first fully turned my attention to this term – 'woke-washing' – scholarly literature on it was significantly scarce. While preparing my talk on 'The "wokefluencers" of "diversity" marketing: the commercial co-optation of free(ing) online labour', for the January 2018 symposium *After Work: Life, Labour and Automation* (Sobande, 2018b), I found myself fixated on understanding the fraught relationship between digital culture, consumer culture, and activism. Although academia's engagement with the notion of 'woke-washing' was lacking at that time, critical discourse on 'wokeness' led by journalists and media professionals was swelling and included discussion of brands' interest in appearing 'woke'.

In the years since then, writing on 'woke-washing' and its contestations has rapidly risen, resulting in a range of explanations that expose the contradictions inherent to the term itself, as well as those at the centre of marketing, academia, and their connections. Perhaps the way that such a term has been (re)framed in academia is symptomatic of 'the contradictions that occur when attempting to develop research that disrupts racial violence while working within and for academic institutions that reproduce racial violence' (Johnson, 2018: 15).

Is 'woke-washing' a useful description of marketers' attempts to position brands in proximity to activism? Is it simply a rinsed and washed-out label that has been leveraged by both marketers and scholars to simultaneously valorize and dismiss the actions of brands, as well as pursue careerist (and capitalist) goals? Perhaps the term 'woke-washing' is always at work somewhere between all those dynamics, with its precise location in flux and impacted by whose perspective of 'woke-washing' is foregrounded, and how the etymology of 'woke(ness)' is (dis)connected from their perception and portrayal of it.

'Woke-washing' is a term that has the potential to be used as part of critical interventions intended to critique organizations and call out their hypocrisy, such as 'the extent to which the commodification of blackness (including the nationalist agenda) has been reinscribed and marketed with an atavistic narrative, a fantasy of Otherness that reduces protest to spectacle' (hooks, 1992: 33). However, 'woke-washing' is also a term at risk of reinscribing some of the very power dynamics that it is intended to critique, such as by being used in ways that merely enable brands (including self-brands) and the capitalist system they stem from. I suspect that 'we' are past the point of the expression's potential recuperation as a critical rhetorical device, particularly as the broader concept of 'wokeness' has been contorted and flung around as part of the circus that is present-day British party politics (Milton, 2022). Perhaps the notion of 'woke-washing' never did the work that it was professed to in the first place?

The body of writing on 'woke-washing' which tepidly critiques brand activity includes claims that '[w]hen brands match activist messaging, purpose, and values with prosocial corporate practice, they engage in authentic brand activism, creating the most potential for social change and the largest gains in brand equity' (Vredenburg et al., 2020: 444). My own approach to analysing the acquisitive dynamics between activism, care, and consumer culture is rooted in a more critical tradition, informed by Black studies and Black feminist work which highlights the oppositional nature of much branding and activism. Put plainly, I argue that brands cannot be activists. If it looks like a brand, talks like a brand, and profits like a brand ... it's a brand.

While significant societal change can indeed occur due to sustained processes of people and organizations chipping away at structural forms of oppression, such work is a far cry away from the ambiguous notion of 'building brand equity and nudging social change' (Vredenburg et al., 2020: 445). The concept of 'nudging' connotes a potential tentativeness, secrecy, or light touch approach which juxtaposes with the clear commitment and robust action that many activists undertake. Accordingly, the term 'activist marketing' (Vredenburg et al., 2020: 445) appears to be an oxymoron. Suggesting that brands can be activists, and defending their efforts to be labelled as such, contributes to capitalism's attempt to consume the radical potential of liberationist work, including by upholding the 'elite capture' (Táíwò, 2022) of 'identity politics' (ibid.).

As cultural anthropologist and documentary filmmaker Marcel Rosa-Salas and I assert, '[t]he epistemic power wielded by the marketing industry and marketing academia, arguably, often entails similar ideological commitments to capitalist political economy' (Rosa-Salas and Sobande, 2022: 177). Such ideological commitments, contrary to what is sometimes claimed by both brands and scholars, include a commitment to the maintenance of brand practices (and resultingly, capitalism). Thus, I am ever sceptical of the implication that brands can achieve 'clear transparency about brand practice and values in support of a sociopolitical cause' (Vredenburg et al., 2020:

444), as the capitalist ideology buttressing branding is in direct opposition with any intention to be transparent about a brand's inner workings.

I am increasingly disinterested in examples of perceived 'marketing success in terms of brand equity, which results from a positive response to the brand driven by strong, favorable, and unique brand associations held in consumers' minds' (Vredenburg et al., 2020: 445). The potentially 'successful' impact of brand equity marketing endeavours is often measured in ways that involve a preoccupation with consumers' perceptions, with little to no consideration of the work and labour experiences of the brands' employees, and the brands' long-term impact on wider society (e.g., socially, politically, environmentally). Essentially, such marketing efforts are often measured using metrics that have little to do with assessing the extent to which a brand is (or is not) aiding forms of societal change that can contribute to tackling specific social injustices.

In contrast with perspectives that promote and praise the notion of 'brand activism', I argue that the concept of 'brand activism' is symptomatic of sustained marketing attempts (in both private and public sectors) to position profit-making activity as radical, and institutions as caring. The fact that writing on 'brand activism' includes approaches that rank this alleged activism, such as Vredenburg et al.'s (2020: 445) slippery scale of 'high to low', symbolizes pervasive, competitive, and hierarchical systems of value which are far from many activist intentions. Contrary to claims that supposedly '[a]uthentic brand activism can be contrasted with the practice of "woke washing"' (Vredenburg et al., 2020: 445), I contend that, akin to the façade of 'greenwashing' (Littler, 2008; Miller, 2017), 'brand activism' is merely a discursive construction that reflects attempts by marketers (and, sometimes, scholars), to capitalize on activism and (re)define it, rather than do or aid it.

For a while now, I have found myself asking:

> are we witnessing the *branding* of "brand activism" occurring, and if so, who and what stands to gain from this? How might academia be complicit in the diluting of radical liberationist politics and the reframing of Black activism to appease marketers and brands (as well as to appease academe)? ... The compulsion across disciplines, spaces, and sectors to support claims of brand activism seems to signal more of a concern with reputational management (on the part of both brands and those who they consult) than a concern with dismantling white supremacy and other forms of entangled oppression' (Sobande, 2021b).

As someone who has and continues to work in both academic and marketing spheres, I recognize that, at times, my work and I may be complicit in such dynamics. So, in writing this book I consider what it means to critique these matters while knowing that neither me nor my work exist outside of the constraints, and capturing gaze and grasp, of capitalism. Among the many prior claims that this book takes to task is the claim that 'woke-washing' is a term that simply encompasses 'inauthentic brand activism in which activist marketing messaging about the focal sociopolitical issue is not aligned with a brand's purpose, values, and corporate practice' (Vredenburg et al., 2020: 445). Such assertions about 'brand activism' and 'woke-washing' appear to miss the point – just as there is no ethical consumption under capitalism, surely, there is no 'brand activism' either.

> 'To me, the potential benefit of critiques of so-called "woke-washing" and alleged "brand activism" is not necessarily the potential to expose the misleading actions of brands or to

imply that such a thing as "brand authenticity" is achievable, let alone measurable. Rather, the potentially generative nature of critiques of alleged "corporate wokeness" includes the clear refusal to uncritically accept rhetoric, representations, and responses by brands which appear to do the work of triviliasing and distorting activism as part of the recuperation of the overall image of the marketplace, not just the image of individual corporations' (Sobande, 2021b).

Conscious of the limitations of merely 'highlighting inconsistencies between messaging and practice' (Vredenburg et al., 2020: 445), in this book I take a different approach to analysing brand adverts and the scholarly study of them. Drawing on Critical Marketing Studies' interest 'in questioning Capitalist values, especially the profit-motive and individualistic conception of "consumer" behaviour' (Tadajewski, 2014: 40), I offer a brief outline of a typology of writing on 'woke-washing', which distinguishes between work which engages with the term to do the following: 1) critique specific brands, 2) critique branding practices and capitalism in general, 3) critique critics of specific brands, and 4) critique critics of branding practices and capitalism in general. Both departing from and building on my prior work on brand 'woke-washing', I theorize the withering and washed-out nature of the term which has often been mobilized in ways intended to help brands rather than spur on structural change.

Further still, I critique

'elements of marketing and consumer culture studies that engage with Black thought and critical studies of race and gender in extractive and acquisitive ways. To be direct, I'm critical of work in these disciplines and areas that results in a cursory nod to Black and racial justice scholarship as part of attempts to position such longstanding work (including that of Black scholars) as something "newly discovered" and "established" by those whose subject position (for example, race, gender, and institutional status) is more palatable to the imperialist, white supremacist, capitalist patriarchal purview of much of academia' (Sobande, 2021b).

Scholarly and industry efforts to maintain and sustain brands include attempts to theorize the relationship between social justice and branding in ways which imply that brands are capable of being radical political actors. As follows, part of the work of challenging the capitalist appropriation of activism is the refusal of narratives such as those of Vredenburg et al. (2020) which, to an extent, are (re)presented as a critique of brand activity, despite perhaps more accurately being described as an attempt to propel and praise it. Unconvinced by Vredenburg et al.'s (2020: 445) positioning of brands as capable of becoming 'activists in the sociopolitical sphere', this chapter considers what political and power relations (within both the predominantly white marketing industry and academia) are part of the process involved in what Vredenburg et al. (2020: 445) refer to as 'when brands become activists', or, as I describe it, when brands are marketed as such.

Unlike the explanation of 'woke-washing' offered by Vredenburg et al. (2020), which asserts that the term describes when 'brands detach their activist messaging from their purpose, values, and practice' (444), I regard 'woke-washing' as an imperfect term with the precarious potential to encompass contradictions inherent to *all* brand activity that is intended to frame brands as deeply invested in activist matters such as racial justice, feminism, and nebulous notions of 'intersectionality' (Rosa-Salas and Sobande, 2022). After all, contrary to what some brands might try to imply, much marketing that is intended to be framed as feminist 'still upholds the profit-oriented idea that women must buy and consume certain products to affirm themselves and the market-bound sense of "feminism" that is being promoted' (Sobande, 2019: 106).

As I have previously argued, when analysing so-called 'femvertising' by brands such as H&M and Missguided, 'a marketing buzz has surrounded the words "intersectional feminism". When incorporated into marketplace activities, the term frequently loses its original meaning, which stressed a commitment to articulating and addressing interlocking forms of structural oppression, particularly as experienced by Black women (Crenshaw, 1989)' (Sobande, 2019: 105). There are many examples of when 'feminist-coded content is effectively and ineffectively used, and discarded, as part of fast fashion marketing messages of inclusivity' (Sobande, 2019: 106).

Founded in 2006, fast fashion company Boohoo has created many adverts that are relevant to discussions about femvertising and my wider interest in investigating the commodification of care. These include the colourful 58 second filmed advert 'HERE'S TO 2022, HERE'S TO YOU', which is viewable through Boohoo's (2022) official YouTube channel and is accompanied by the following explanation: 'We have big goals for 2022. As the new year rolls in, we're pledging to use our reach to drive positive change and to inspire confidence and body positivity'. The advert opens with a bubblegum pink background and the canary yellow words 'hey you', and 'yeah you', which establishes Boohoo's direct and informal address of the audience.

Boohoo's 'HERE'S TO 2022, HERE'S TO YOU' advert also includes written words such as 'Everything we do is made possible because of you' and features a montage of images of different people wearing Boohoo clothing, including a shot of someone in lingerie, who appears to have stretchmarks on their stomach. Another part of the advert features a visual of a Boohoo billboard with the statement 'all bodies are *billboard* ready' – perhaps partly as a critical commentary on a controversial and banned 2015 Protein World billboard advert which featured a very slender and bikini-clad model, and asked 'are you beach body ready?'. Among additional written statements in the Boohoo (2022) advert are the following:

> we're here to support you, we are here to … empower and inspire you … help you to achieve your dreams … remind you to take care of your mind and body … give back to our community … raise awareness and funds for good causes … and continue our journey towards a more sustainable future.

Shortly after the half-way mark, the advert features the instructive and, possibly, spiritual sounding words, 'it's time to realise your potential … realise your worth … realise that your power is just being you'. Such messaging is consistent with aspects of popular feminist perspectives that circulate as part of the 'economy of visibility' that Banet-Weiser (2018) has prolifically researched and written about. What appears to be the advert's recognition of the COVID-19 crisis involves statements such as 'it's been a tough few years but now it's time to go to that party … dream big, apply for the job, wear the outfit … and be unapologetically you'.

In Boohoo's advert, consumption experiences, such as fast fashion ecommerce transactions, are positioned as playing a part in a so-called 'return to normal' (e.g., 'now it's time to …'). The advert's message about 'empowerment' appears to rest on an assumption that the target audience is lacking in confidence (e.g., 'be unapologetically you'), or dealing with some sort of self-esteem deficit, as is indicated by Boohoo's paternalistic tone (e.g., 'it's time to realise your potential'). The advert's mention of career aspirations (e.g., 'dream big, apply for the job') and words such as 'worth', also hint at how societal expectations of productivity are part of the everydayness of 'normal' life.

As Jenny Odell (2019: 1) argues in *How to Do Nothing: Resisting the Attention Economy*, '[n]othing is harder to do than nothing. In a world where our value is determined by our productivity, many of us find our every last minute captured, optimized, or appropriated as a financial resource by the technologies we use daily'. Picking up on such a theme, Chapter 3 examines how marketed discourses of productivity, home life, and presence have been prolific during the pandemic, in ways that are often distinctly classist, racist, and ableist.

Overall, Boohoo's 'HERE'S TO 2022, HERE'S TO YOU' advert may be an attempt to communicate that they care about driving 'positive change' and supporting 'good causes'. Yet, other than referring to 'body positivity', and alluding to hollow '#GirlBoss' feminism, there is little evidence of them explicitly articulating what such causes and forms of change are. The advert appears to present Boohoo as taking a stance, but does so in ways that are relatively, and, maybe, strategically, ambiguous. The marketing messages present in Boohoo's 'HERE'S TO 2022, HERE'S TO YOU' advert reflect how some brands have claimed to care during the COVID-19 crisis, and tried to cultivate camaraderie, but in ways that tiptoe around naming exactly what it is that they care about.

The notion of brands taking a stand is often based on the assumption that this entails a clear socio-political (and, *sometimes*, financial) commitment on the part of brands. However, brands may carefully choose their words in ways that result in the illusion of their investment in certain people and issues, in the form of messages that use buzzwords, but do not clarify exactly who and what it is that they (claim to) care about. As well as being a potential example of 'femvertising' and the fraught relationship between marketing and feminism (Maclaran et al., 2022), this Boohoo advert may be regarded as a form of 'carewashing' – an expression that refers to examples of 'how powerful business actors' (Chatzidakis et al., 2020: 891) have 'been keen to promote themselves as "caring corporations" while actively undermining any kind of care offered outside their profit-making architecture' (ibid.).

Boohoo has faced publicly documented claims of exploitation and mistreatment, and in 2020 announced an independent review following allegations of dangerous working conditions and labour exploitation in its UK supply chains (Drapers, 2020). When accounting for their potentially contentious work and labour practices, Boohoo's invocation of notions of empowerment and care appear to be particularly galling. Their 'HERE'S TO 2022, HERE'S TO YOU' advert is part of a longer recent history of Boohoo marketing and femvertising. That history includes their 2017 '#AllGirls' campaign which, again, featured messages such as 'keep on being you', but was critiqued due to the disconnect between Boohoo's claims of inclusivity and the notably limited nature of the diversity of people in the campaign.

Sustaining sentiments that were evident in their previous adverts, the message of Boohoo's 'HERE'S TO 2022, HERE'S TO YOU' is one of self-celebration, but also, embracement of a return to 'normal' life, or a rise of the seemingly 'new normal'. The advert's message hinges on the idea that consumer culture is the key to 'empowerment', and that brands (Boohoo) care about *you* – even though 'greenwashing' efforts do not obscure the destructive socio-environmental impacts of the fast fashion world that they are part of. Such advertising is consistent with popular feminism's themes of 'empowerment, confidence, capacity, and competence' (Banet-Weiser, 2018: 3), which are, arguably, wrapped up and tenuously tied together with allusions to – or, even, illusions of – intersectionality (Rosa-Salas and Sobande, 2022). Despite this, some people may still view such a brand and their actions as an example of 'brand activism'.

When writing about the contested concept of 'brand activism', Vredenburg et al. (2020: 446) refer to when 'a brand adopts a nonneutral stance on institutionally contested socio-political issues, to create social change and marketing success', but I ask – change to what end, for whom, and with what intention? My questions concerning this are shaped by Critical Marketing Studies 'concerned with challenging marketing, concepts, ideas and ways of reflection that present themselves as ideologically neutral or that otherwise have assumed a taken-for-granted status' (Tadajewski, 2011, p. 83). So, I argue that the notion of brands taking a 'nonneutral stance' in response to societal issues is *not* evidence of their alleged 'activism' – far from it. As an example of what I mean, there is a stark difference between being anti-racist and simply claiming to not be racist. Still, both positions have the potential to be referred to as a 'nonneutral stance' – but are they both indications of activist inclinations? I think not.

Being (and being described as) 'nonneutral' drastically differs to being (and being described as) political, or an activist. Marketing scholarship that frames the alleged 'nonneutrality' of brands as an activist credential, reduces activism to little more than a label or badge of honour that papers over the cracks of a brand's public image. In fact, it could be argued that – despite what some brands claim – brands have never been neutral, so it is inaccurate to suggest that them adopting a 'nonneutral stance' deviates from industry norms or is akin to activism.

Adverts, such as Boohoo's 'HERE'S TO 2022, HERE'S TO YOU', are part of a history of femvertising which involves brands dipping in and out of discourse on empowerment, popular feminism (Banet-Weiser, 2018), and what schol- ars Shani Orgad and Rosalind Gill (2022) term 'confidence culture'. But creating and circulating femvertising does not a feminist make. Such approaches to marketing, which increasingly involve brands trying to portray themselves as 'inclusive' of Black women, are sometimes part of efforts 'to detract from scandal surrounding their ethics and CSR' (Sobande, 2019: 110). To date, '[a]s fast fashion brands try to survive mounting backlash that the industry faces, including on issues of sustainability and labour ethics, femvertising and diversity marketing remains a potentially alluring CSR diver- sion strategy' (ibid.).

Also, as the work of Maclaran et al. (2022: 1) highlights, the future of the relationship between marketing and feminism is one that is destined to be shaped by ongoing and '[f]ast growing online grassroots activism' – work which brands may seek to capture or replicate, but, hopefully, will struggle to. Rather than assisting 'aspiring brand activists' (Vredenburg et al., 2020: 444), my hope is that this part of Chapter 2 helps to develop ongoing analyses of the dynamics between activ- ism and consumer culture.

My critical approach involves (dis)regarding 'brand purpose' and 'brand values' as terms that do not do much other than refer to the fact that brands claim to care about certain matters. This is one of the reasons why I reject the idea of 'the authenticity of brand activism' (Vredenburg et al., 2020: 445), which has been dubiously defined as when 'the alignment of a brand's explicit purpose and values with its activist marketing messaging and prosocial corporate practice – emerges as being critically important for marketing success as well as potential for social change arising from this strategy' (ibid.).

Instead of leaning into discourses of so-called 'brand activism' and the construct of 'authenticity', I turn away from vague and competition-oriented claims that 'brand activists may strengthen outcomes in an increasingly crowded marketplace' (Vredenburg et al., 2020: 444). So, I work with partly flawed and fruitful expressions such as 'femvertising' and 'woke-washing', and accompanying terms such as 'brand pretense' to pick apart the ways that both the marketing industry and academia are invested in alluding to brands' assumed activist credentials – including their alleged capacity to care for / about more than profit.

There are clear tensions between scholarly efforts to sanitize brands' (in)actions, and those intended to critique brands and, more pertinently, the capitalist system that spawns them. Such tensions appear in the form of who and what is referenced and / or omitted in the rush to establish what so-called 'woke marketing' and 'brand activism' is, and in the form of what use of the term 'woke-washing' tends to involve being critical and / or supportive of.

Frankly, territorial marketing and consumer culture studies (which is not how I would describe this whole area of work but needs to be named) repackage various ideas and concepts (including by extracting and decontextualizing Black scholarship and activism), to try to possess terms and remove the potential for them to critique this field of research and the marketplace that it examines. I contend that the insistence on using terms such as 'brand activism' and 'woke marketing', and claims that 'woke-washing' is a derogatory descriptor, form branding and public relations tactics, on both individual (e.g., self-brand) and institutional levels. Use of these terms can be part of a strategic approach to naming and / or claiming that reveals more about proprietorial behaviours that underpin academia and the marketing industry, than indicating that there is any evidence of brands' efforts to address structural oppression.

Moving away from an explicit focus on 'woke-washing', and towards a deeper analysis of how brands have claimed to care during the COVID-19 crisis, the next section of this chapter considers how messages about multiculturalism have been communicated in the content of marketing. Such discussion is followed by writing on the marketization of higher education, which involves revisiting my contemplations on 'brand activism', and their connections to the commodification of care.

CONSUMING (UN)COMFORTABLE MULTICULTURALISMS

Since 2020, there has been ample evidence of brands 'framing the current COVID-19 global pandemic as a force that is bringing people together, in ways that may distract from their dubious treatment of employees, as well as their thirst for productivity and profit' (Sobande, 2020a: 1034). While brands' attempts to signal a sense of togetherness have sometimes been subtle, in other cases, they have overtly attempted to invoke 'team spirit', such as by connecting to sports events and constructions of national identity, culture, and pride.

Food delivery company Deliveroo released their 'England 'Til We Dine' Euro Championship advertising campaign in the summer of 2021, which acknowledged their sponsorship of the England football teams. The 'Creative Works' section of *The Drum* (2021a) features a profile on 'Deliveroo: England 'Til We Dine by Pablo', which refers to it as being a brand campaign that 'builds off the insight that even though we're England fans, minds will also be on favourite takeaways and food from different countries around the world'. When critically considering this campaign, it is helpful to remember the work of bell hooks (1992: 21) on how '[t]he commodification of Otherness has been so successful because it is offered as a new delight. More intense, more satisfying than normal ways of doing and feeling'. It is also essential to engage the work of Manzoor-Khan (2022: 84) which emphasizes the grim state of the UK defining 'extremism as "opposition to" British values', resulting in the perception that 'racial Others arguably pose a criminal threat until we learn them' (ibid).

A 30-second filmed advert formed the locus of the Deliveroo campaign and alludes to aspects of 'the politics of multiculturalism' (Hesse, 2000: 5) in the UK, namely, within England. Analysis of the advert illuminates some of the many ways that brand messages about multiculturalism and national identity are entangled with the claim that brands care – but about whom, and what?

At the time of writing this, Deliveroo's 'England 'Til We Dine' advert has had more than 78,000 views via their official YouTube channel. The advert features a voiceover by presenter, comedian, actor, and producer Karl Pilkington, who opens filmed footage by listing a range of food from different places – pork bao, lamb dhansak, and chicken taco. Therefore, the advert immediately alludes to multiculturalism, which is a term that 'always refers contextually to the "western" and "non-western" cross-cultural processes involved in establishing the meanings invested in the racially marked incidence of contested cultural differences' (Hesse, 2000: 2).

In 'England 'Til We Dine', between meals being reeled off by Pilkington are punchy chants of 'England!', which drown out Deliveroo's potential pitch to appear invested in different countries, cultures, and the people who are part of them. Despite the relatively short length of this advert, the content of it seems to capture aspects of 'national cultural formations' (Hesse, 2000: 5), including connections made between cuisine, consumption, comfort, and cultural inclusivity and / or diversity.

Specifically, Deliveroo's 'England 'Til We Dine' campaign reveals some of the ways that marketing in the UK during the COVID-19 crisis has involved brands seeking to convey a sense of community and camaraderie, while actively invoking nationalistic sentiments which may be comforting to some but undoubtedly exclusionary to others. The advert is one of many discussed in this book which signal how brands and marketing practices construct and respond to 'the nation's imagined communities' (Hesse, 2000: 1) by trying to comfort them while encouraging them to consume.

My use of Hesse's (2000: 2) term 'nation's imagined communities' is not intended to dismiss the existence of people and cuisines from many different cultures and countries in England, and Britain more broadly. Instead, I engage with the concept of national imagined communities to acknowledge forms of framing and (re)imagining which are part of perceptions of who and what constitutes countries, cultures, and national identity – including what it means to be 'England 'Til We Dine'.

Pablo (2021), the creative agency behind the 'England 'Til We Dine' campaign, describes it with words such as the following:

> Pablo and Deliveroo's new Euro's 2021 campaign brings to life the insight that whilst we're all about supporting the England team during the football, when it comes to match-day dining we're less loyal and enjoy all manner of amazing cuisines from around the world. As fans across the country are cheering on England, we know that their minds will also be on their favourite lamb dhansak, pork bao, brioche buns and tacos.

Pablo's use of words such as 'loyal' arguably signal how the campaign depends on discourses of dutifulness that are tethered to nationalistic notions of support and team spirit. Their focus on the enjoyment of food also evidences how the campaign is meant to conjure up feelings of comfort, perhaps under the guise of claiming to care about different cultures and their peoples.

The visual content of the 'England 'Til We Dine' advert includes mouth-watering shots of hot meals, such as pizza boxes covered with an Italian flag print, which gesture to multiculturalism, or, at least, cultural difference. As well as focusing on food, the advert includes scenes that feature the familiar faces of famous England football players – Harry Maguire, Jack Grealish, Dominic Calvert-Lewin, and Tyrone Mings. A recurring visual in the advert is that of the England flag (derived from Saint George's cross) which is symbolized in various ways, including the strategic placement of cutlery, and the deconstruction of food, which results in visuals that resemble the flag.

In other words, although Deliveroo's advert involves optics that point to the Other (different cultures, cuisines, and multiculturalism), it is English patriotism and celebration of it that is the most salient theme. This results in what I deem to be hollow messages of multiculturalism which are firmly embedded in praise of England, assumptions about people's 'normal' food consumption habits, and the premise that 'to seek an encounter with the Other, does not require that one relinquish forever one's mainstream positionality' (hooks, 1992: 367), in this case, one's Englishness. Just as British 'values themselves are racialised as white' (Manzoor-Khan, 2022: 84), seemingly so too are the values of English patriotism invoked in Deliveroo's advert, regardless of how 'colourful' or 'exotic' it may appear to be.

Hesse's (2000: 2) work on 'inward-looking nationalist identities' is highly relevant to this analysis, as such writing clarifies how nationalist identities and the marketing of them can involve deep investments in so-called 'good' (and patriotic) citizenship, including perceptions of loyalty to a nation-state. The scholarship of Ben Carrington and Ian McDonald (2001) on *'Race', Sport and British Society* is also essential to engage here. As they argued near the start of the second millennium, 'sport is a particularly useful sociological site for examining the changing context and content of contemporary British racisms, as it articulates the complex interplay of "race", nation, culture and identity in very public and direct ways' (Carrington and McDonald, 2001: 2). When absorbing such observations, it is apparent that Deliveroo's 'England 'Til We Dine' campaign presents a cornucopia of representations and rhetoric that are rich with sport (and food) signs and symbols which are suggestive of what Carrington and McDonald (2001) observed.

At first glance, meanings associated with multiculturalism in the 'England 'Til We Dine' advert may appear to contrast with statements such as those captured by the generatively critical words of Hesse (2000: 3), 'No multiculturalism, please – we're British'. Yet, the 'England 'Til We Dine' advert falls short of foregrounding multiculturalism or different cultures in ways that divest from English patriotism. Parts of Pilkington's narration particularly point to this, including the lines 'Our hearts are England crazy. Our mouths are more jalfrezi', which may hint at the notion of being emotionally invested in England but merely carnally interested in (cuisine from) elsewhere.

Adverts such as Deliveroo's 'England 'Til we Dine' exemplify how brands have sought to conjure up a sense of comfort during the COVID-19 crisis, including in ways that connect to messages of multiculturalism, but which ultimately affirm nationalistic patriotism. The work of hooks (1992) on 'Eating the Other: desire and resistance' significantly informs my analysis of the 'England 'Til We Dine' filmed advert, and the wider campaign it is part of. hooks (1992), who explores the relationship between racism, white supremacy, and capitalism, observes that commodified 'fantasies about the Other can be continually exploited, and that such exploitation will occur in a manner that reinscribes and maintains the status quo' (367) – including via marketing that alludes to the 'normality' of multiculturalism but also upholds patriotism.

hooks' (1992) analysis includes discussion of how the commodification of Black culture involves efforts to make blackness 'the "spice that can liven up the dull dish that is mainstream white culture"' (14). Deliveroo's 'England 'Til we Dine' advert is an example of how brands attempt to allude to multiculturalism to create such a sense of 'spice'. The assortment of meals that the campaign depicts – from calabrian pepperoni to prawn szechuan – is part of how English patriotism is porously positioned as being inclusive of people, or, at least, food, from a variety of different countries. Still, the closing lines of the advert perfectly encompass what seems to be the campaign's investment in appealing to those who take pride in England, more so than maintaining messages of multiculturalism.

An animated fish leaves the viewer with what is perhaps meant to be, dare I say, a comforting reminder that when using Deliveroo 'you can have fish n' chips n' all!'. Whether the light-hearted line is meant to provide relief to those who may be completely disinterested in 'Other' food from elsewhere is unclear. Irrespective, the sustained emphasis on England and its norms is entirely apparent in the advert.

In addition to featuring a filmed advert, the overall 'England 'til We Dine' campaign includes radio and social media activity, as well as the launch of edible face paints which were intended to provide people with the opportunity to decorate their face or their food. Evidently, eating, and other forms of consuming, are at the centre of the campaign. This could be regarded as an expression of how brands seek to frame forms of transactional consumption as a celebration of cultural difference – in ways that are consistent with the notion of 'consumer citizenship' (McMillan Cottom, 2022).

You might be asking, what does all of this have to do with the commodification of care during the COVID-19 crisis?

A lot. Although Deliveroo's advert does not explicitly refer to 'caring', its illusion of inclusivity insinuates that caring about England means caring about, or, at least consuming, aspects of multiculturalism. The advert's tone connotes some of the celebratory and commodified invocations of multiculturalism that Hesse (2000) critiques.

'Multiculturalism refers to particular discourses or social forms which incorporate marked cultural differences and diverse ethnicities. In this "substantive" sense, multiculturalism can be named, valued, celebrated and repudiated from many different political perspectives' (Hesse, 2000: 3). The allusions to multiculturalism in Deliveroo's advert seem to be symptomatic of what hooks (1992: 25) referred to as being 'cultural strategies that offer Otherness as appeasement, particularly through commodification'.

The 'England 'Til We Dine' advert is the by-product of a brand recognizing the potential profitability of upholding nationalism while marketing perceived symbols of multiculturalism (e.g., food from 'elsewhere'). Also, the advert may be perceived as part of the 'pick 'n' mix' of marketing during the COVID-19 crisis, which attempted to tap into notions of togetherness and 'team spirit' in ways that obscured the ongoing impact of deep-rooted inequalities.

Related examples of how togetherness has been leveraged in this way include the 'Appeal from Roger, Asda's CEO: We're all in this together' [2020] video, as well as the 'We're all in this together' videos of Fitbit [2020], M&S [2020], and Disney Channel UK [2020]. Moreover, '[t]he comments of celebrities such as American singer-songwriter Madonna, who has claimed that "coronavirus is the great equalizer", convey a similar sentiment and the damaging perspective that this crisis is being universally experienced, in the same ways, by all' (Sobande, 2020a: 1034).

Wide-ranging evidence highlights that contrary to proclamations that 'we're all in this together', certain demographics have been disproportionately impacted by the pandemic and the crises that preceded it. 'The persistence of intersecting structural oppressions and socioeconomic disparities is laid starkly bare when considering the disproportionate impact of COVID-19 on Black people of African descent and Asian people in Britain who have been critically ill coronavirus patients' (Sobande, 2020a: 1036). This includes the experiences of individuals 'who work in high-risk roles that are [temporarily] identified as "key" and "essential"' (ibid.), even though due to racism, classism, xenophobia, and sexism, some of these roles (e.g., working in cleaning and hospitality) were previously seldom societally deemed as 'skilled' (Cowan, 2021).

Despite such inequalities, many brands have created campaigns during this time (2020–2022) which depend on vapid messages of unity, community, and caring about cultural diversity, without acknowledging distinct differences between the material conditions and harms faced by people during the COVID-19 pandemic. Regardless of brands' efforts to move away from the language of racism and xenophobia, towards the ambiguity afforded by terms such as 'difference' and 'diversity', '[w]hat has been central to the experience of black people in Britain has been neither the "idea" nor the "politics" of "race" as the "idea" or the politics of "racial difference". Rather, it has been racism and other forms of oppression' (James and Harris, 1993: 3).

When accounting for stark differences between people's experience of the crisis, including how racism and racial capitalism are implicated in this, the cynical gestures of brands who seek to construct camaraderie and conjure comfort through messages of multiculturalism, seem reductive. Lines uttered during the narration of Deliveroo's advert, such as 'we're St George, head to toe', accompany a shot of a bulldog sporting an England football top and St George printed hat. This is yet another example of the overall campaign's intention to cultivate patriotism. Such patriotism is partnered with hints at heroism, as is evident in the words of Pablo (2021), the creative agency behind the campaign and who describe the advert as '[t]he hero film' which 'features the England team and Karl Pilkington, who voices a fun subversion of the traditional football song "England 'til I Die".'

Discourses of heroism and nationalism have featured in branding strategies for a very long time (Aronczyk, 2013; Jiménez-Martínez, 2021; Lury, 2004; Preece et al., 2019; Sobande and hill, 2022), including in the world of sport (Carrington and McDonald, 2001), so it is unsurprising to encounter such sentiments in the content of marketing during the COVID-19 crisis. However, what makes this Deliveroo example revelatory in terms of what the advert suggests about the commodification of care, is both the content of the advert and the contemporary context that drastically contrasts with it.

Vitriolic anti-Black comments and actions were directed at England football team players Marcus Rashford, Jadon Sancho, and Bukayo Saka following the outcome of the European Championship final in July 2021. The three players whose penalty spot kicks were not successful were subjected to a torrent of racist abuse and threats of violence, including on social media platform Twitter. This all occurred little more than a year after galvanizing Black Lives Matter (BLM) activism which was visible around the world in response to the murder of George Floyd by a police officer in the US, as well as the deaths of many other Black people due to police brutality and violence (Grier and Poole, 2021; Taylor, 2021).

As author, academic and broadcaster Emma Dabiri (2022) describes it, '[m]uch of the energy that erupted after the murder of George Floyd seems to have been hijacked by a brand of "antiracism" overconcerned with microaggressions, with representation in film and media, and with interpersonal relationships. It's a framework that largely ignores economic inequality, or the potential for strategic, organized struggle'. Thus, in the months that followed a rise in media and public discourse on BLM in the UK, '[a]cross various sectors, brands pledged to "hire more Black people" and claimed they would "amplify Black voices", and "diversify" their industries' (Sobande, 2020c).

One of many examples of how BLM impacted different actions in the UK includes the fact that at the start of the European Championship 2020 final (which, due to COVID-19, took place in 2021), the England team took the knee. Such a potentially anti-racist gesture is intended to be a statement in support of Black people. Even though the final opened with a somewhat collective statement about the need for racism to be addressed, it ended with an ongoing wave of online and offline racist abuse aimed at Black football players on the England team, including by people in England. When witnessing such vile, and, sadly, predictable, abuse unfold, I recalled Deliveroo's advert 'We're England 'Til We Dine', which is based on a message that seems to imply that English patriotism and multiculturalism are not mutually exclusive.

The allusions to cultural inclusivity that underpin 'We're England 'Til we Dine' contrasted with watching Black England football players being harassed by people who may proudly profess to be 'England 'til we die'. Then again, arguably, given Deliveroo's emphasis on celebrating cultural difference insofar that it satisfies a patriotic English audience, maybe their advert does not contrast at all with what followed the Championship final in 2021[1].

Here, it is helpful to turn once more to Tyler's (2020: 26–27) research which critically examines 'the crafting of stigma in the service of governmental and corporate policy goals, and the cultivation of stigma to extract political and economic capital'. Perhaps part of the function of Deliveroo's 'We're England 'Til we Dine' advert is to implicitly stigmatize critique of English patriotism (and stigmatize dissent in general), which in this marketplace context is linked to a brand's (Deliveroo's) pursuit of 'economic capital' (Tyler, 2020: 27).

---

[1] In July 2022, 'the Lionesses' (England's women's football team) won the Euro 2022 football tournament. This was a momentous occasion which resulted in commentary concerning the often overlooked, underpaid, and societally obstructed efforts of women in football. Accordingly, there were many collective calls for changes to be made to address inequality in the sport. While the success of 'the Lionesses' was indeed cause for celebration for many people, it is important to acknowledge the racism, sexism, and misogyny that was, *and* still is, directed at players of African descent on this team. Thus, while this chapter highlights the racism and online abuse that was directed at players such as Marcus Rashford, Jadon Sancho, and Bukayo Saka in 2021, this should not be mistaken for negating the abuse that Black women football players face too.

'By its nature, sport is a complex protean cultural formation. It is too simplistic to argue that sport improves "race relations", just as it is to say that sport can only reproduce racist ideologies' (Carrington and McDonald, 2001: 2), but events that followed the European Championship final in 2021 certainly bring home (as if it ever left ...) that racism is as English as the fish and chips featured in Deliveroo's campaign. Any meaningful interpretation of the 'We're England 'Til We Dine' advert, and any advert for that matter, must grapple with the socio-political context it is part of. Regardless of the rhetoric and representations deployed in 'We're England 'Til we Dine', racism and xenophobia is ever-present and societally normalized in England, and in Britain more broadly.

It has been claimed that '[t]he notion of post-imperial Britishness – as a legal, civic, inclusive non-racial identity – has eased this absorption of millions of people of different backgrounds, religions and ethnicities' (Cowley, 2022). However, the (dis)connection between the sentiments of 'We're England 'Til we Dine' and the aftermath of the European Championship final in 2021 indicates that 'post-racial' perspectives of national identity and nationalism in Britain are redundant. Undoubtedly, racism and colonialism continue to contour Britain, including patriotism and the treatment of people within, and beyond, this place.

I don't think that anyone is expecting a Deliveroo advert to put an end to inequalities in Britain, and my critique of this advert is certainly not based on the assumption that Deliveroo intended to actively address racism and / or xenophobia. Still, I shine a light on this specific example because it reflects a larger landscape of advertising during the COVID-19 crisis, which illuminates some of the ways that brands have tried to portray themselves as relatable with the use of depictions and discourses of togetherness, comfort, and the myth of multiculturalism which is always overshadowed by the pervasiveness of patriotism.

Having so far predominantly focused on advertising and marketing messages that stem from the private sector, I now move on to consider how the branding practices of an aspect of the public sector (UK higher education) are also part of the commodification of care during the COVID-19 crisis. Focusing on the marketization of higher education, I consider some of the key components of content and campaigns created by universities as part of their effort to appear to care about certain socio-political issues (e.g., the gender pay gap and the Black degree-awarding gap). Undeniably, my thoughts and theorizing on these matters are shaped by my own experiences of working in UK higher education – previously in marketing and communications for several years, and then as a scholar since 2015. That said, the analysis that follows is informed by a range of writing, research, and work on the neoliberal university (Breeze et al., 2019), particularly, critiques of its (mis) treatment of people (both students and staff) from structurally marginalized demographics.

WHEN UNIVERSITIES (CLAIM TO) CARE

In their crucial edited collection on the neoliberal university, scholars Maddie Breeze, Yvette Taylor and Cristina Costa (2019: 1) reflect on how UK universities have been altered by 'the principles of "free market" capitalism – particularly the logics of profit, individualism and competition'. Breeze et al. (2019) provide examples of this in action, such as the fact '[i]t is well established that *the* university is subject to and implicated in the reproduction of market logics, often identified in the tuition fee regime of England and Wales' (1–2). Although many universities portray themselves as bastions of efforts to address inequality, their brand image cannot mask the power relations that form the foundations of much of UK higher education.

Extensive work has critiqued 'the role of academia in (re)producing white supremacy' (Kamunge et al., 2018: 2), and posed pressing questions such as 'What does it mean to stand as an academic witness against the function of white supremacy within and beyond the walls of the academy?' (Johnson, 2018: 16). Those who have addressed such issues include The Surviving Society Podcast (hosted by Chantelle J. Lewis and Tissot Regis, and executive produced by George Ofori-Addo), which explores 'local and global politics of race and class from a sociological perspective', and who 'are resistant to positioning such projects as anything other than a collective endeavour, but are also mindful that, as Black creatives, podcasters and academics, their method and praxis can be overexposed to processes of co-option, plagiarism and erasure' (Lewis et al., 2021: 94).

Inspired by crucial work, such as that of Johnson (2018) and The Surviving Society Podcast (Lewis et al., 2021), this section of Chapter 2 critiques how UK higher education responded to the surge in discourse about BLM and anti-racism in the Spring / Summer of 2020. But, before examining this, it is important for me to establish key aspects of the current state of many UK universities, where both staff and students have been navigating the impact of COVID-19 (and multiple crises) on their lives, including their 'classroom' experiences and expectations.

As scholars Yvette Taylor and Kinneret Lahad (2018: 2) note, due to the marketization of universities, '[m]any colleagues, departments, disciplines and institutions are under constant threat of being closed down, forced to downsize, lay off staff, and justify their existence according to rigid market-driven models'. Among numerous issues in UK higher education is the persistence of pay gaps (e.g., the gender pay gap and the race pay gap), as well as the continued use of precarious and casualized work contracts.

'While precariousness refers to employment status in the first instance, it also has an emotional dimension. Not knowing where the next paycheck is going to come from, not knowing what may happen in the longer term, not having adequate sick pay or a pension – this produces feelings of insecurity' (Dowling, 2021: 2). At the time of writing this, 'around half of teaching-only staff and 68% of researchers are employed on fixed-term contracts, while many more have contracts which are dependent on funding' (UCU, 2021). Also, 'UCU's [the University and College Union's] research showed that 42% of staff on casual contracts have struggled to pay household bills, while many others struggle to make long-term financial commitments like buying a house' (UCU, 2021).

While precariousness and structural inequality is undoubtedly a major issue in UK universities, it is essential that work which is intended to address these matters does not frame hardships faced in higher education in a way that trivializes people's experiences of precariousness and inequality in other sectors and environments where, on average, they have fewer rights and receive less pay. Also, any discussion of precariousness and inequality in higher education which does not account for the experiences of individuals in cleaning and hospitality roles in this context, is a discussion that likely discounts issues concerning classism and its intersection with other forms of oppression.

As someone who has worked in UK universities (although, not exclusively) for over a decade, what seems to have remained consistent is the normalization of structural racism, sexism, xenophobia, classism, and ableism, as well as other interconnected oppressions. Such forms of oppression impact both students and staff, including PhD researchers who are often both at once (e.g., postgraduate research students who are graduate teaching assistants), and whose experiences of precariousness can include being under pressure to do work even when they are unwell. Despite the 'divide and rule' discourse of universities that seeks to stoke tension between students and staff, the discontents of both groups are often strikingly similar and connect to issues such as inadequate provision of resources and mistreatment by these institutions. For this reason, and many more, it is vital that the health and wellbeing of both university students *and* staff is structurally supported.

UK higher education disparities between workload, pay, and work conditions, seem to be as common as garden-variety weeds. Hence, one of numerous ongoing campaigns undertaken by the UCU (2021) is the 'four fights dispute', which is intended to tackle such matters. Specifically, the demands of the 'four fights dispute' include calls for 'fair pay', 'job security', 'manageable workloads', and 'equality'. Continuing with my considerations of 'femvertising' and how brands position themselves as empowering women, I now examine aspects of how universities have claimed to care (and about whom) during the COVID-19 crisis. Specifically, I reflect on the yearly waves of universities posting International Women's Day (IWD) messages on social media platforms such as Twitter. In 2022, following the IWD posts of many UK universities, their hypocrisy was called out by the Twitter profile Gender Pay Gap Bot

(@PayGapApp), which Francesca Lawson and Ali Fensome are behind (Lawson, 2022).

The Gender Pay Gap Bot on Twitter is currently followed by approximately 241K people and features a bio that includes hashtags such as '#InternationalWomensDay', '#PayGapDataDay', and '#BreakTheBias'. A website that the bio links to provides a more detailed explanation of the Gender Pay Gap Bot – '[t]he totally automated Twitter account that spent International Women's Day annoying your social media and comms teams' (Gender Pay Gap App, 2022). More precisely, '[w]henever a company listed on the government's gender pay gap service tweets International Women's Day key phrases, The Gender Pay Gap Bot automatically responds with their median gender pay gap' (ibid.), which is based on publicly available data. The overview of what the Gender Pay Gap Bot does outlines an intention to 'provide a neutral, factual counterpoint to emotion-led International Women's Day social media posts' (Gender Pay Gap App, 2022), such as IWD 'messages of "empowerment", "inspiration" and "celebration"' (ibid.) which contrast with the reality of many women's lives.

The theme of IWD in 2022 was '#BreakTheBias', which many UK universities posted about on social media, including by sharing images of women with their arms crossed, forming an 'X' shape as a statement about the need to 'break the [gender] bias'. Such messages, and the wider communications campaigns that they were part of, exemplify how universities claim to care (e.g., about *some* women).

As I mentioned, shortly after the proliferation of UK universities' IWD posts, the Gender Pay Gap Bot responded by highlighting the median gender pay gap of the institutions that had proudly posted. Then, some UK universities tried to prevent people from commenting on their original posts by changing their 'who can reply' tweet settings, presumably to mitigate the potential for people to critique the contrast between their IWD comments and their grim gender pay gap. The speed at which the Bot responded to university IWD posts, paired with the poignancy of the pay gaps pointed out, made a dent in IWD discourse that was intended to market universities as caring about equality, and, particularly, caring about women.

Lawson (2022) states that '[b]y contrasting companies' sentimental words with cold hard data, we've helped the public see through these empty gestures and start holding companies accountable for their gender pay gap', but the question of whether universities will now do more to tackle such pay gaps remains to be answered. While UK universities sought to suggest they are supportive of women on IWD in 2022, many women were facing the ongoing impact of sexism, misogyny, and interconnected forms of oppression such as homophobia, transphobia, ableism, ageism, Islamophobia, colourism, classism, and racism, which result in significant differences between the experiences and material conditions of women in higher education. Typical university IWD narratives overlook such differences, including the experiences of Black women who face some of the sharpest edges of labour market precarity and structural oppression (Sobande and Wells, 2021).

Empty university statements about equality, bias, stereotypes, and inclusivity, are often accompanied by images and / or videos of smiling (typically, white, but, sometimes, tokenized Black and brown) faces. This is suggestive of who society deems to be 'normal' and 'respectable' women. Seldom do universities' IWD posts acknowledge the experiences of trans women, or the rampant nature of transphobia in UK higher education and the society it is part of. Also, such IWD marketing messages tend to obscure the realities of women affected by the intersections of the race, gender, *and* disability pay gaps, such as by using broad terms, including 'equality', without naming specific and interconnected inequalities that impact women, but not only them.

As well as posting social media and marketing content on IWD and gender equality, in recent years (particularly since 2020) UK universities have shared comments in response to Black Lives Matter (BLM). Research suggests that most UK universities responded publicly to BLM, such as in the form of showing 'solidarity by releasing a statement on their website and then sharing that on their social media as they took part in the #blackouttuesday social media trend (which had organisations and individuals post a black square and stop using social media for 24 hours to show support)' (Halpin, 2020: 4). The university doth protest too much, methinks.

The #blackouttuesday social media trend that occurred in 2020, which cut across many spaces and sectors, was eventually the subject of much criticism due to the potential for such posts to distract from vital BLM-related information being shared online, as well as the capacity for such #blackouttuesday content to have the effect of simply platforming the people and institutions who were posting it. Some of the statements issued by universities in response to BLM have been strongly criticized, as '[m]any believed that the statements were hollow because anti-Black racism is not a new phenomenon – over the decades, students, staff and activists have been raising these issues – yet it appeared that only now universities were prepared to talk about their support of Black lives publicly' (Halpin, 2020: 4). The Halpin (2020: 2) report on *UK Universities' Response to Black Lives Matter* high-lights elements of the (Western) international context within which universities sought to suggest they were anti-racist, or, at least, not racist:

> The murder of George Floyd on May 25th 2020 triggered a worldwide response and boosted the momentum of the Black Lives Matter (BLM) movement. Society was asked to acknowledge that it is not enough to be non-racist; everyone has a part to play to help society become actively anti-racist. As with other key sectors, higher education is being held to account by its core constituent groups, with students, staff and the wider community all asking universities to consider their part in systemic racism, and what they can do to be truly anti-racist.

The various ways that UK universities responded to such matters included producing new reports on race equality, holding one-off panel discussions, and attempting to 'diversify' the curriculum. The research of Halpin (2020), which involved a survey and interviews with students, staff, activists, and student officers in UK higher education, explored such people's perception of how universities responded to Black Lives Matter. Halpin's (2021: 2) key findings included 'that only 26% of survey respondents felt that their university's response to Black Lives Matter was appropriate or sufficient'. Such dissatisfaction with these responses is unsurprising for many reasons, including when considering the words of Johnson (2018: 17) who documented having 'seen so many panels and group discussions with all white academics talking about how we must take a stand or speak truth to power, with no discussion of how these institutions (and the bodies normalized within them) are deeply implicated in the functioning of that power'.

The notion that UK universities care about Black people is to some, laughable, particularly given the litany of experiences and evidence of anti-Blackness in UK higher education. There is an extensive list of examples of how universities fail, if not actively obstruct, Black people – from the workload, pay, contract, and work condition disparities faced by Black staff, to the 'degree-awarding gap' that impacts Black students who are often unsupported. Documentaries such as 'Is Uni Racist?' (BBC, 2021) have investigated students' experiences of racism, including how their lives have been harmed by forms of abuse and surveillance. Even a quick search of Freedom of Information (FOI) requests faced by universities reveals extensive interest in the realities of the experiences of Black students and staff, which are experiences that universities can often conveniently obfuscate under the guise of General Data Protection Regulation (GDPR) concerns.

The marketization of UK higher education has resulted in institutional embracement of the language and logics of markets – 'recruitment strategies', 'reputational risk', 'brand cohesion and consistency'. Since my days of working at the Universities and Colleges Admissions Services (UCAS) events, and Open Days as a university communications assistant, UK higher education has become more caught up in the online attention economy. It seems that 'social media is reshaping universities' value systems in a scramble for likes and shares' (Carrigan, 2021) and due to their compulsion to convey that they care. Universities' attempts to project, protect, and preserve their (brand) image include the way that they comment on IWD and BLM, and how they do (or do not) create the opportunity for people to respond to such comments. Such communications activity is, to me, a clear example of elements of the commodification of care, and, of course, not only during or due to the COVID-19 crisis.

Many universities put a lot of effort into trying to get people to buy into them (both literally and figuratively). Such efforts include universities' work to present themselves as caring about different demographics and societal issues – from Black people during Black History Month in October to women on International Women's Day in March. Universities' claims to care, if conveyed in ways that are well-received, may be regarded as part of how they pursue capital and one way that they seek to stand out from the higher education crowd in the race to recruit more (and more, and more ...) students. Caring, in this case, is a marketable trait that institutions attempt to ascribe themselves as part of their work to appear to be more than (just) a brand. It is not that care is the commodity. Instead, care is (re)constructed, consumed, or captured (Táíwò, 2022) by universities as part of marketing approaches based on higher education's culture of commodification.

In other words, universities' claims to care (about IWD, BLM, and everything in between) are not a commodity for sale. However, such claims symbolize one of the ways that universities seek to sustain their reputation and, possibly, distance themselves from marketization via messages of equality, diversity, and inclusion that tend to demarcate who and what they regard as 'respectable'. Arguably, much of university marketing (not only about IWD and BLM) reflects the 'controlling anxieties' of universities.

Controlling anxieties is 'a term that encompasses expressions of the anxieties (and in turn, expectations, and norms) of institutions, such as their concerns regarding reputational management and the (un)controllable nature of their public image' (Sobande, 2022a). The controlling quality of such anxieties includes 'their capacity to convey the conventions and preoccupations of institutions in a threatening, or, at least, cautionary, way – including by indicating what they deem to be "deviant" behaviour in need of "disciplining" (and the individuals who they deem to exhibit it)' (ibid.).

I'm not sure whether any UK universities would (have the audacity to) view themselves as activists, but regardless of that, what is apparent is that many use the lens of social justice in ways that may distract from the commodification processes that they are part of, and in ways that unintentionally illustrate their controlling anxieties. Although universities work hard to construct and constantly communicate their brand 'voice', including by carefully posting about social and political issues on social media, perhaps they have much to learn from the timelessly haunting 1990 lyrics of Depeche Mode – sometimes, people 'enjoy the silence'.

CARING (OR, CONSUMING), TOGETHER?

'For decades, brands have used rhetoric and representations with the aim of yielding adverts which feature emotional appeals. Often, such efforts are intended to humanise brands and make them relatable and attractive to different target demographics' (Sobande, 2020a: 1034). I opened this chapter by reflecting on the power of advertising which appeals to people's emotions and gets them to care (e.g., about the product and / or service and the brand behind it), so it seems right to close it by reflecting on a campaign that is strategically sentimental in its style. Since the emergence of the COVID-19 crisis there has been a slew of brand efforts to stir emotions and touch on a form of togetherness that often upholds the idea that brands are 'one of us'. This is demonstrated by advertising campaigns such as 'It's a People Thing' by British banking brand Halifax, in addition to the other examples discussed in detail throughout this book.

'It's a People Thing' 'seamlessly amalgamates various vignettes, capturing the highs and lows of those living on a typical British street' (*The Drum*, 2021b). Featuring the track 'Stand By Me' by Oasis, the filmed advert depicts different emotional moments in people's lives. These include someone receiving flowers (captioned 'it's a joyful thing'), a couple commiserating together while looking at a pregnancy test result (captioned 'it's a we'll try again thing'), sisters trying to film a workout video that goes wrong (captioned 'it's a sister thing'), and a child looking lovingly at their pregnant mother (captioned 'it's a new playmate thing'). Other scenes in the advert include a teary-eyed person looking lovingly at a dog that seems to be waiting to be euthanized at the vet (captioned 'it's a thank you, for everything'), and an elderly couple looking lovingly at a photograph of a child after an adult outside waves to them while on a run (captioned 'it's a look what we achieved thing'). Although it is not clear who the child in the image is, the elderly couple's gaze of admiration alludes to it potentially being their child or grandchild.

The advert closes by focusing on a Halifax branch, and the narrator states 'for the ups, the downs, and everything in between … Halifax, it's a people thing'. Overall, the advert is illustrative of 'emotional appeals in advertising banking services', which is a phenomenon that the work of marketing scholar Emmanuel Mogaji (2018) sheds light on. Such advertising by Halifax, which appears to simultaneously individualize notions of care while drawing on the themes of togetherness, 'nuclear' family life, heteronormative coupledom, and (middle-class) domesticity play a common part in UK marketing depictions and discourses in general. 'It's a People Thing' particularly focuses on pregnancy and parenthood, which may be part of a strategy to position the brand as practically being part of the family. As the advert opens with a bird's eye view and closes with a relatively brief, but clear focus on the Halifax brand, it may suggest the ever-present nature of Halifax (e.g., watching over people, and never far from where they are).

Adverts such as 'It's a People Thing' may be intended to communicate messages about caring for each other, and, caring, *together*. However, by nature, such adverts are clamped to consumer culture which (re)presents consumption and commerce as care. 'It's a People Thing' might be yet another example of what Chatzidakis et al. (2020) call 'carewashing', but, specifically, it is an example of how when claiming to care, brands push messages about so-called 'normal' life – including by repeatedly depicting the pursuit and pride of parenthood, which connects to the discourses of (re)productivity which I now move on to discuss in Chapter 3.

3

DISTRACTION, DREAMING, AND ANGST

I've been thinking a lot about the word 'distraction' lately.

Sparked by my own experience of long Covid (including 'brain fog' – see Chen, 2014) and ADHD, I've found myself reflecting on the details of what defines 'distraction' and accompanying ideas about 'inattentiveness'. I guess you could say I've been 'distracted' by 'distraction' and all the layers of power at play within how this word can be wielded and weaponized.

Funnily enough, while thinking about all of this I often found myself 'distracted' from my plan to write some of these thoughts down – and my plans to write this book. I eventually came to view the time and process it took me to get to the point of penning these words as being part of the necessary pacing and pausing that was (and still is) part of me reflecting on 'distraction', 'focus', and 'dreaming' (as well as critiquing the messages of productivity pushed in society, including in the content of adverts).

The difficulties I faced when trying to find these words can't fully be captured by referring to dealing with 'distractions' or being prone to be 'distractable'. Rather, some of such difficulties connect to the stifling feeling that I had to find the *right* words, before articulating anything on this topic at all. I was feeling the push of societal pressures to possess and perform 'comprehension – a word that suggests both finality but also wholeness of grasp – something that feels impossible when brains are foggy' (Chen, 2014: 172–173).

Just as societally 'distraction' often becomes the nemesis of 'focus' (and, consequently, productivity), I was sometimes viewing my own use of words via a reductive oppositional binary lens of 'the right words' (a.k.a., potentially achieving clarity and the illusion of certainty) and 'the wrong words' (a.k.a., exposing my uncertainty and anxieties in ways that might 'distract' from what 'I'm trying to say' or may leave me feeling vulnerable).

By the time I came to write these words, and particularly due to ongoing conversations about Black presence, time, and pacing with Black (and) Muslim geographies scholar Azeezat Johnson, as well as the words of photographer Oluwatosin (Wasi) Daniju, and decolonial studies scholar Katucha Bento, I realized that my original plan to find the *right* words before writing about 'distraction', 'focus', and 'dreaming', was premised on the fragile idea that there are words that encompass all that I'm trying to say and share here ... when maybe there aren't.

Previously, I had been trying to move past or through the 'messiness' of my thoughts and reach a point when I felt I could communicate them in a way that might 'make sense' to others and feel less scattered than my mind. In essence, maybe I had been grasping for a way to 'present' my thinking that might mask its unfinished, always in flux, and frequently fraught nature. However, many Geographies of Embodiment (GEM) Research Collective[1] conversations led me to think differently about how I was thinking and hoping to write about 'distraction'.

In society, 'distractions' and 'being distracted' and / or 'distractable' are often discussed in a manner that positions 'distraction' as being something inherently negative and in need of being overcome. The work of Odell (2019) comes to mind when writing about this, including the statement 'I am opposed to the way that corporate platforms buy and sell our attention, as well as to designs and uses of technology that enshrine a narrow definition of productivity and ignore the local, the carnal, and the poetic' (xii).

'Distraction' is so often known as an obstacle to topple when in pursuit of focus (and the forms of valorized (re)productivity that such focus is sometimes thought to inevitably lead to). Under a capitalist system, the poetic becomes framed as distraction and, even, *feeling* becomes a distraction to distinguish. While writing these words I am hyper-aware of the various distractions that I am attempting to dodge. Background sounds that crescendo and tease my ears. The many objects and colours that surround me in both comforting and (over)stimulating ways. The grooves and texture of the desk that my laptop rests on, and the assortment of felt-tip pens to the right of the laptop. There is no doubt in my mind that I'm writing this piece while feeling distracted and anticipating the next moment

---

[1] The Geographies of Embodiment (GEM) Collective is a community of public scholars demanding and embodying liberation. More information about the GEM Collective is available at: www.gemcollective.org (accessed 22 July 2022).

when I find myself chasing a thought, memory, or a sense long enough to disrupt the flow of my writing before finally finding my way back to it (and myself) again.

Reading and learning more about 'distraction' and 'distractibility' has involved me commonly coming back to the question of 'distracted from and / or by what?'. What if I'm distracted by something that brings me pleasure and joy? What if I'm distracted from traumas of the everyday in ways that involve self-preservationist forms of escapism that are really ways of feeling and staying grounded? Again, when posing these questions, I do so with an acute awareness of how issues regarding 'distraction' and 'distractibility' present significant problems in people's lives. Without diminishing that, and by drawing on some of my own understandings and experiences of 'distraction', I am curious about continually exploring the implications of when something perceived as not resulting in, or obstructing, (re)productivity, is societally regarded as a (destructive) 'distraction' by default.

There are times when dreaming (in the broadest sense of the word) is dismissed as mere 'distraction' because it is not interpreted as being of value to what hooks (1992) refers to as imperialist, white supremacist, capitalist patriarchy. There are times when both wandering and wondering is compartmentalized as 'distraction' and 'detour' in ways that undermine forms of *being* that depart from following the (productive) path most trodden. What *is* 'distraction', and how does who attempts to define what it is and why, reveal much about society's pre-occupation with 'perfecting' the 'ability' to 'focus' (and stay focused!).

Me mulling over the way the notion of 'distraction' can function in society is not at all intended to dismiss the realities of 'distraction' faced by many people, including, but never limited to, those who are neurodivergent and neurodiverse. Instead, my hope is that by thinking through how ideas about 'distraction' are sometimes operationalized, my writing might contribute to efforts to push back against the constant pressure to 'produce' (and perform productivity and perfectionism), which underpins much of society. Then again, I recognize the contradictory nature of the fact that in articulating this, I am engaging in a form of productivity (writing a book), but I am doing so in a way that feels reflective of the simultaneous nature of experiences of 'hyper-focus' and 'distraction' that can be part of some people's experience of ADHD.

A question such as 'am I distracted or am I allowing myself to dream?' can be a flippant one, particularly if asked by a person who has not had terms such as 'distraction' and 'inattentive' directed at them as part of diagnoses or ableist assumptions. Also, the notion that 'distraction' and 'dreaming' are sometimes interchangeable terms may be an unhelpful one that is connected to compulsions to deny the very real challenges presented by the former ('distraction') by simply repackaging it as the latter ('dreaming'). So, with all this in mind, I'm not sure where my experiences of 'distraction' and 'dreaming' start or end, that is, assuming they can ever even be understood in that way. Maybe 'distraction' and 'dreaming' always exist outside of, and beyond, time and measurements that are typically imposed on people's lives (Jones, 2022).

Here, I am reminded of the book *The Fire Now: Anti-Racist Scholarship in Times of Explicit Racial Violence*, edited by Azeezat Johnson, Remi Joseph-Salisbury, and Beth Kamunge (2018). Such work includes the resonant words of Derrais Carter (2018: 40) on 'Black study': 'Blackness somehow remains both in and out of time, pushing against the attempts to be ordered in the present, revisiting and reimagining the past, and producing future possibilities'. How might Black experiences of 'distrac-tion' and 'dreaming' – or as Jones (2021b: 825) powerfully describes it, 'black dream geographies' – be part of all that Carter (2018) evocatively describes? Time is far from being experienced in the same way by all people, and as the writ-ing and scholarship of Nadine Chambers (2019) on 'Black and Indigenous Geographies' demonstrates in detail and with care, 'Sometimes Clocks Turn Back for Us to Move Forward'.

This section of my book might be perceived by some as being 'in defense of distraction' or 'in defense of dreaming', or *both*. My thoughts and feelings on various framings and (de)valuations of 'distraction' and 'dreaming' are unsettled, but in ways that, for now, I'm at relative peace with, rather than trying to 'push through'. This is partly due to what I have learnt from the deep and uplifting work of Jones (2021b: 825) – *thank you, Naya* – on 'meanings of dream or sleep in Black/African American epistemologies', which takes seriously the intricacies of Black interiority. Does my 'distractibility' contribute to when, how, where, why, and with whom I dream? Are my dreams 'distracting' me, and if so, from what, and why does that matter? These are questions that I will continue to spend time with, and which will no doubt change in ways influenced by where my mind wanders, as well as how others dare to dream.

Sharing my thoughts on 'distraction' and 'dreaming' may seem to be a bit of a random interlude in this book, but such writing is part of how I convey my thinking on a range of concepts and experiences that relate to care (and, its com-modification). When embarking on this book project, I always knew that I would write about discourses of productivity that have been a part of marketing messages about work and COVID-19, but it also felt important to make time and space to articulate the messy interiority of life (e.g., experiences of 'distraction' and 'dreaming') which brands tend to gloss over or glamourize.

While critiquing the promotion of (economic) productivity by brands during the crisis – which the aspirational expression 'levelling up' is part of – I sought to pause and parse some of the ways that dreaming, detouring, and distraction, play both enriching and unsettling roles in people's lives. 'There is a radical possibility in the moment of collective pause, particularly when faced with the imperialist white supremacist capitalist patriarchal pressure to constantly produce' (Sobande and Emejulu, 2021: 2), but the capacity for people to experience such a pause is impacted by the intersections of racism, sexism, classism, and other interlocking forms of oppression. In sum, when writing this book, I wanted to avoid being so focused on commenting on the market logic of productivity that I failed to acknowledge some of the different experiences, encounters, and emotions that have affected people's lives during the COVID-19 crisis and the many crises that it connects to.

I believe that some brands have attempted to present themselves as more invested in moments of pausing and parsing than productivity, including by playing with relatively slow-paced poetry and spoken word which can create a dream(y) like quality in adverts, and which contrasts with the speed of capitalism's cogs. Such tactics have increasingly been evident in the content of adverts for banks that are jostling to be perceived as homely, rather than harassing, and personable, rather than solely profitable. However, despite the growth of such a marketing approach, messages about productivity (e.g., how to work 'better' and for longer) are still pervasive. Accordingly, during the process of writing this book, while listening to online music playlists I encountered many adverts about how to learn to read faster (e.g., Speechify).

Although much of this chapter involves analysis of marketing messages about productivity, if there is one thing that people take away from it, my hope is that it is a sense of how despite institutions' insistence on (hyper)focus and (re)production, as well as their attempts to manage and monitor people, vital forms of dreaming, distraction, and angst prevail. Beyond this book, I will continue to keep thinking (and, maybe, writing) about how 'distraction' and 'focus' is often distinguished between in ways that involve people being discouraged from dreaming and detouring away from the relentless pressure to produce and perform that punctuates much of the world. In addition, I will continue to critically reflect on how such a binary distinction between 'distraction' and 'focus' connects to the ways that structurally marginalized people are simultaneously and societally chastised for 'doing too much' and 'not enough'. But now, I further examine the part that marketing and advertising plays in pushing messages of productivity that present people as a mere means to a (mostly monetary) end.

DEPICTIONS AND DISCOURSES OF PRODUCTIVITY

Messages about maximizing your productivity during the pandemic have appeared almost everywhere – from trite Twitter posts about turning past-times into profit, to billboards that boast about the benefits of a 'rise and grind' mindset. The idiosyncrasies of influencer culture include the amplification of these messages of productivity, such as content about the constant need and pressure to produce more content, which, inevitably, leads to expectations and the production of – *you guessed it* – more content. Stating this is not intended to be a criticism of the fact that some people's source of income is based on content creation, nor am I implying that the work of influencers and content creators should have come to a grinding holt during the COVID-19 crisis. My comments are intended to be more of a critique of the societal persistence of messages to constantly, and quickly, produce more (and more, and more, and ...), and how the impatient attention economy of digital culture feeds into that (Odell, 2019).

I seek to avoid dismissing the digital work and labour of people, including influencers and content creators, and some of whom have faced financial precarity due to the impact of COVID-19. But I also acknowledge that aspects of influencer culture can glorify precarious and contingent forms of work and labour and can push the painfully passé message that 'anyone can make a living from this!', when the reality is that the influencer culture industry is anything but a meritocracy (Duffy and Hund, 2019; Glatt and Banet-Weiser, 2021). As well as reflecting on this, it seems pertinent to name the fact that, on occasion, the commercial content and promotional work of influencers is rather arbitrarily assumed or expected to be a form of activism and / or resistance (Sobande et al., 2022).

To recall the #blackouttuesday response to BLM (referenced in Chapter 2), many influencers took to platforms such as Instagram to simply post black squares. Nevertheless, such meagre engagement with the topic of BLM was sometimes praised, although was also often considerably critiqued. I mention this example because it is a reminder of how the content that influencers produce is sometimes politicized in ways that paints 'fake deep' content, or well-meaning but vacuous posts, as a catalyst to change. Also, some of such #blackouttuesday activity, and related creation and amplification of content about BLM, seemed to entail what I have referred to as being '[t]he celebrity whitewashing of Black Lives Matter and social injustices' (Sobande, 2022b: 130), which is when 'white celebrities' efforts to call out and critique whiteness and social injustices can in fact have the effect of reinscribing the dominant and marketable status of whiteness' (ibid.).

On the topic of online discourse, early in the pandemic I remember raising an eyebrow at branded content that claimed to help people to 'make the most' out of their 'pandemic experience' by acquiring new skills to stand out from the (job market) crowd. Although many people were struggling to survive, marketing messages that positioned the pandemic as an opportunity to produce (profit) and the 'perfect time' to pursue parenthood, constantly popped up and pressured people to keep their foot on the pedal of (re)productivity – and in ways that clearly connected to cis-heteronormative notions of gender, coupledom, and family life.

Over these last couple of years, sometimes it felt as though I couldn't take a cursory glance at many online platforms or publications without being confronted by statements about the assumed optimal conditions for peak (re)productivity, including the ideal amount of sleep and the much sought-after surroundings to fuel work and / or foster fertility. Such messaging often seemed to specifically speak to middle-class people whose experiences of work and leisure are such that, to an extent, they / we can determine where and when to work.

The work of those involved in 'Solidarity and Care' (2020) – 'a public platform supported and produced by *The Sociological Review*' has stressed how the intersections of race and care impact 'the lived [including work] experiences, caring strategies and solidarity initiatives of diverse people and groups across the globe during the COVID-19 pandemic'. For many people dealing with dangerous work environments and unpredictable shift patterns, including as 'key' or 'essential' workers during the COVID-19 crisis, there was no time, space, or support to pursue the sort of conditions that are claimed to sustain (re)productivity (not that anyone should have to be pursuing such conditions and their assumed outcomes anyway!).

Despite the dismal fact that many people in low-paid and unpaid work faced unsafe and often hostile environments during the pandemic (including unsustainable workloads and pressures to constantly leave their homes), various institutions still waxed lyrical about lessons in pursuing productivity from the 'comfort of your home'. Such messages often made clear brands' assumptions about what a home is / looks like / and feels like, or, at least, what the homes of their target audience (should) consist of.

Both before and during the pandemic, marketed notions of 'normal' home life in the UK have often involved 'scenes of predominantly white familial domesticity and food consumption' (Sobande and Klein, 2022: 8), as well as the reinforcement of cis-heteronormative familial relations. What seems to be less common 'is meaningful depictions or acknowledgment of the experiences of people who live on their own or are isolated … people who are houseless, people in care, and people who have had to work in spaces outside of their home' (ibid.) during the COVID-19 crisis. Although the well-worn saying goes 'home is where the heart is', the adverts of many brands suggest that home is where the immaculate beige interior, 'nuclear' family, make-shift gym, and 'nutritious' meal (which are framed in fatphobic ways that stress the potential for certain foods to mitigate 'COVID weight gain') is.

Of course, depictions and discourses of home life and productivity have been around a lot longer than the COVID-19 crisis has, but the nature of this pandemic has impacted such messaging in ways that are worth analysing. For example, as Arzumanova (2021: 2) affirms, during this time, 'the luxury design industry's entreaties to (re)design our homes to accommodate a newly public life led in private amounts to a symbolic suburbanization founded in the fear of "contaminated" racialized bodies'. Also, as Horgan (2021) reminds readers when writing about the COVID-19 crisis, '[d]espite the rhetoric about "essential workers" and "key workers", those who had to continue to work in person were not only those whose jobs could reasonably be deemed "essential". Just over half of people continued going to work' (1–2), and commonly 'it was up to employers to declare whether their companies did essential work' (ibid.).

Focusing on themes related to home, working life, and notions of (un)essential productivity, this section of the book offers insights related to topics including brand marketing and workplace imaginaries, as well as advertising and societal constructions of productivity. Without dismissing the tangible and material realities of work, I outline aspects of the relationship between imaginaries and ideas about work (e.g., *where* it takes place, *how* it is experienced, and *who / what* benefits from it). Namely, I critique how brands have drawn on workplace imaginaries in ways that reflect what type of work, and whose experiences of it, tend to be societally praised in capitalist settings such as the UK.

Since the pandemic took force in 2020, swiftly followed by government enforced 'lockdowns' and 'social distancing' measures, marketing that promotes economic productivity has often been coupled with content concerning whether people are more productive when 'at home' or 'in the office' – overlooking the fact that some people's office or workspace was 'at home' or not tied to one specific site long before the pandemic.

Marketing, media and public discussion about productivity and the pandemic has coincided with discourse on workplace settings, including perceptions of employees' presence and / or presenteeism at work. The deluge of headlines on the topic of work during these times include 'Millions are more productive while working from home, study finds' (Ross, 2020) and 'The post-pandemic productivity mirage' (Babb, 2021).

Often, employers have sought to monitor and manage employees in invasive ways which range from systematically surveilling their social media profiles to demanding that they keep their webcam turned on during all online video meetings. Also, in some cases, employers have made ableist 'assumptions about the perceived wellness and whereabouts of employees based on online optics and their (in)visibility' (Sobande, 2022c), which 'can, at times, be oppressive and insensitive to difficult domestic settings' (ibid). Of course, work takes place in many different spaces and does not always involve an employer. However, at the cold heart of some marketing attempts to evoke emotional connections to work, seems to be disrespect of work–home boundaries, and an emphasis on the idea of the office, including the (non)hierarchical social relations that it spawns.

Brand pontifications about the productivity of people and how much such individuals seem to (dis)like their place of work include Dettol's viral 2020 advertising campaign, which is filled with material to analyse when seeking to explore how brands have simultaneously framed themselves and working life during the COVID-19 crisis. The campaign seemed to be intended to frame the experience of returning to office workplace environments as something to look forward to after lockdowns. It even appeared to romanticize the mundanity and tedium of many experiences of work, such as commuting to an office, where, as Dettol (or McCann who created the campaign) put it, there are 'Water cooler conversations. Proper bants …'.

Some people critiqued such messaging 'for appearing too similar to a government return-to-work campaign' (Small, 2020). The Dettol campaign seemed to involve an effort to remind people of what they apparently missed or enjoyed about office working life, but the tone of it completely clashed with the fact that many people did not long for the (work)days of supposedly '[t]aking a lift. Seeing your second family'. More than that, Dettol's in-joke style campaign emphasized the idea that people feel emotionally connected to their place of work, and, by extension, their employer(s). Unsurprisingly, such marketing messages were responded to with backlash.

As people were quick to point out, the adverts that Dettol's campaign consisted of were based on a set of assumptions that overlooked the fact that many people felt pressured to return to various (and often, unsafe) spaces during the COVID-19 crisis – including office environments. Statements that featured in adverts that formed the campaign included 'The boss's jokes. Plastic plants. Office gossip'. Such content read like a weird shopping list and invoked images that may be at odds with the daily working lives of a lot of individuals.

Some people said that Dettol's advert seemed to be attempting to mimic the punchy style of the iconic 'choose life …' introduction to Irvine Welsh's book (turned into a 1996 film) *Trainspotting*. On Twitter, Welsh himself weighed in on the online critique of Dettol's approach (Small, 2020), speculating about the possibility that the campaign was created by someone with a Conservative political position, perhaps because the advert may be perceived as parroting the party line of the UK government.

The workplace imaginary invoked by Dettol involved an emphasis on using public transport and stepping back into 'the office' in a celebratory, and even grateful, way. As such, it, arguably, ignored the experiences of many people, including those of individuals who are chronically ill, disabled, and are clinically extremely vulnerable to the impact of COVID-19, but whose lives have been treated with disdain throughout this crisis (and long before it too).

Dettol's campaign encouraged workers to 'disinfect surfaces we use throughout the day, so we can do it all again tomorrow' (McGonagle, 2020). Although that message may have been created to focus on ways to maintain hygiene and the cleanliness of spaces with the use of Dettol, it also promotes forms of productivity that people were pressured to sustain in ways that put their health (and lives) at risk during the pandemic (e.g., 'so we can do it all again tomorrow'). Additionally, such messaging obscures the fact that many (mostly, working-class) people have had to work outside of their homes throughout the pandemic, including to clean the buildings of 'office' workers who were able to work remotely for a certain, if not, indefinite, amount of time.

Of course, during the COVID-19 crisis, Dettol were not the only brand that created a campaign which pushed messages about productivity and work. Still, what may have made their decision to do so particularly irksome is that their product is not one that is inherently linked to ideas about working life. What I mean by that is, unlike brands such as LinkedIn whose image is inextricably connected to ideas about employment – and who launched their #InItTogether campaign in 2020 (Sobande and Klein, 2022) – during the COVID-19 crisis Dettol made the decision to actively associate themselves with workplace imaginaries, in ways that back-fired. *Campaign* even asked the question '[w]ill Dettol's "back-to-work" ad campaign damage its brand?' (Small, 2020). While I'm certain that Dettol's brand image will remain relatively intact and stand the test of (at least, some) time, the backlash that they faced has likely left a stain that may be difficult for them to remove.

As I mentioned at the start of this chapter, although there is discussion of marketed discourses of productivity throughout it, I also try to make time and space to reflect on different experiences, encounters, and emotions that have been part of how people have been 'processing' the COVID-19 crisis. As a result of this approach, I now move on to my thoughts (and notes) on memories, which involves outlining some of the ways that memories have been moulded by the clutches of consumer culture during the first quarter of the twenty-first century. Adverts such as those of Dettol involve the use of workplace imaginaries that are (re)presented as memories of experiences of work, but as I now focus on in more detail, despite capitalism's efforts to control memories (e.g., how they are made, expressed, understood, and archived), there is a lot more to them than the mirage that is marketed.

DIAL M FOR THE MIRAGE OF MEMORIES

The Notes app on my iPhone is both magic and mess. It is a jarring and eclectic mix of stream-of-consciousness writing and unfinished notes that bring me back to both painful and peaceful points in my life. Probably much like many other people, my Notes app houses old shopping lists, abandoned attempts at poetry writing, and a random assortment of words that paint a pastiche picture of my (former) self:

Refreshing, refreshing

refreshing

to see

what words have been

spat

and crash

landed between

the comments of curious souls ...

– 26 March, 2019

Each time I revisit the Notes app and scroll through my previous scribbles I notice something new. I am vulnerable with myself in that space, or at least, it seems that way. I spot when the frequency of my notes changed, and I remember the undulating pace of life in the past. I come across thoughts of mine that are at once familiar and distant to who I am today. I delight in rediscovering recommended music and books that I had noted in haste when parting ways with friends. I pause, still taken aback by the hours I spent exercising when trying to outrun the torments of life. I reflect on the time that it took me to draft and continually redraft something that seemed so significant *then*, but now feels freeing in its emptiness.

My Notes app is brimming with fragments of ever-changing yet always present memories that amount to a mirror of sorts. Somedays the reflection I see looking back is a comforting one. Others, it is a reminder of deeply distressing difficulties that, despite not always being visible to all, continue to impact my life today. As the work of scholars such as Daniel Clarke (2020) brings to life, digital technology and media is sometimes interwoven with memories that are part of experiences of grief. As Clarke (2020: 1) writes, in the vivid piece 'First my dad, then my iPhone: an autoethnographic sketch of digital death', '[p]otentially lousy singing and research poetry are used to make sense of losing – soon after he died – my iPhone containing video footage of my father singing'.

As the work of Clarke (2020) indicates, much has changed since Alexander Graham Bell was hailed for inventing and patenting a germinal telephone in the nineteenth century. Although it was once an exclusive and somewhat immobile item that few could access with ease, the telephone is now often homed in the pockets of people on the move. The portability of mobile phones that emerged in the twenty-first century troubled the telephone's status as a firm fixture in various domestic and public spaces. No longer were phones solely deemed to be a way of communicating with others at a distance. Instead, they were praised for providing people with the power to browse the web, make music, capture images, navigate themselves when lost, and perhaps above all, play.

The concept of a 'home phone' began to fray and experiences of memory-making and ephemera were altered with the inception of mobile apps. Whether it is via an iPhone Notes app or other diary-like functions, such phones have become digital journals where (some) people write and record their fleeting thoughts, in-depth musings, and in some cases, ingenious ideas. The arrival of the smartphone, which has both mobile telephone and computing functions, shifted understandings of the purpose and practicalities of phones. Sometimes near to weightless, smartphones seem a far cry away from cumbersome corded telephones that require people to physically dial numbers. By now, for decades smartphones have offered individuals the opportunity to document, share, and even edit, snapshots of their lives with others, including pictures and videos of everyday moments of domesticity.

Even long before the development of smartphones, the telephone was a portal through which to engage with other people and places. However, depending on your vantage point, the digitally enabled affordances of mobiles and smartphones have enhanced and / or undermined crucial communication and connections between people.

For some separated by seas, the touch of a smartphone button helps them to experience a sense of being at home, together. Still, particularly propelled by societal moral panic, others may regard such phones as aiding self-representations and interactions that are at odds with the development of meaningful relationships. So, smartphones, or more precisely, different uses of them, are fraught with tensions between the potential to enrich, hinder, and harm lives. They are objects that are associated with togetherness and introspection. Such phones also symbolize the temporariness of consumer trends (remember 'flip phones'?) and the enduringness of human needs and desires to connect with others.

As well as containing self-archived photo albums that may invoke a comforting nostalgia and be interpreted as examples of self-expression, smartphones manufacture memories. Some functions of smartphones even involve, what I view to be, the construction of a mirage that is manipulatively marketed as a memory. Information available at www.support. apple.com includes writing about 'Use memories in photos on your iPhone, iPad or iPod touch'. Such writing refers to the Memories function as enabling people to rediscover moments from within their photo library due to the way that their iPhone can recognize significant people, places, and events there.

iPhone Memories are described as being curated collections that are presented due to this so-called recognition of significant people, places, and events. These Memories, I argue, are not memories at all. Rather, they are an uncomfortable remixing and repackaging of images, footage, and audio taken and saved on digital devices, and which amount to people paternalistically being told who / what / how / and when to remember.

'Remixing is an open-ended and non-linear process that always involves both a nod to the past (what came before which is being remixed) and the development of something different that captures part of the present (the ongoing outcomes of the remixing process)' (Sobande and Emejulu, 2021: 1). Unlike forms of digital remix culture that involve individuals intentionally (re)creating work and playing with the possibilities of remixing practices, the types of remixing that are part of functions such as iPhone Memories (re)present forms of corporate capturing as creativity.

Understandably, some people may feel as though this Memories function is just a bit of fun that sparks laughter or brings a smile to their face. But there is much to lose by ignoring its intrusive nature and solely deeming it as a source of entertainment. Just as smartphones have enabled people to communicate with others in dynamic ways, they have provided ruthless corporations with the chance to (further) monitor those who use their products. And as the Memories function suggests, these smartphones and their power to track have helped corporations attempt to appear as though they intimately know the people who use these items. Such phones may create an illusion of intimacy and privacy, but this does not equate to the absence of disquieting processes that involve people constantly being observed and surveilled in ways shaped by racism, classism, sexism, xenophobia, and other intersecting oppressions.

There is an eeriness to the iPhone Memories function. Such eeriness is especially pronounced when the function leads to someone being confronted with an unsolicited montage of images, animated footage, and audio that depicts or connotes a loved one that is no longer 'here' or represents events and a specific time that is connected to trauma. The agency that exists in elements of how people make memories, and recall them, seems to be stripped away by the Memories function.

iPhone Memories ultimately eclipses the warmth and randomness that can be a core component of some people's recollections. The phone function essentially serves up something uncomfortably cold that more closely resembles hard-sell advertising tactics than the serendipitous or intentional experience of remembering. Nevertheless, not all aspects of how smartphones operate, and are used, are as unsettling as Memories.

Interviews that informed my research regarding *The Digital Lives of Black Women in Britain* highlighted the significant ways that smartphones are used as part of the play(fulness) that propels Black digital culture and diasporic connections, in addition to the creative production of Black media and political consciousness-raising work (Sobande, 2020e). In the words of someone who chose the pseudonym Ruby, 'people are just making their own spaces … it's very DIY … with our iPhones. Making our own iconography and making our own content … it's really important that we carve out our own narratives and that we don't shy away from creating spaces for ourselves'.

As Ruby's words allude to, unlike the static quality that was once attributed to the telephone, smartphones have become tools that can facilitate different types of making, and impactful efforts to bring about social change, such as by disrupting the British media status quo and foregrounding perspectives that are frequently dismissed by the mainstream press: those of Black women. Yet, the processes of producing which smartphones can enable (e.g., writing, designing, collaborating) tend to involve those who use such smartphones experiencing oppressive forms of capturing, tracking, and surveillance that are not always perceptible but are incredibly powerful.

The opportunity to make something with a smartphone is often contingent on providing corporations with information that will be used in ways that entrench existing power dynamics and inequalities. Thus, as well as being perceived as digital devices that can be used to communicate and create, smartphones are best understood as capsules. They are indigestible containers of details that become known as data – media that is algorithmically framed as memories, and time that is warped by the blending of synchronous and asynchronous interactions and experiences of intimacy. No amount of aesthetic appeal and design detail can distract from the datafication activity at the core of much smartphone use.

Since the global coronavirus (COVID-19) pandemic emerged, which resulted in the enforcement of 'lockdown' laws and physical 'social distancing' in the UK between 2020–2022, the central role of phones in many people's daily lives has been heightened. Such phones simultaneously serve as lifelines and sources of misinformation and disinformation. Hence, political and media messaging during the pandemic has urged people to use mobile and smartphones to access resources that may be essential to survival, while also encouraging them to exercise caution and fact-check when encountering information about coronavirus via social media and messenger apps.

It is important to contextualize these events by acknowledging that despite their relatively wide availability in marketplace settings, someone's access to mobiles and smartphones should never be assumed. Due to distinct disparities between people's material conditions, mobiles and smartphones are far from being used by everyone. Regardless of this, an emphasis on mobile and smartphone communication can crop up in media, political, and public conversations concerning the coronavirus pandemic, such as reporting peppered with terms such as 'pre-pandemic' and 'post-pandemic' which point to how the coronavirus crisis is defining understandings of what constitutes the recent past ('the time before …').

Because of the life-altering impact of the pandemic, suddenly, certain photos saved on smartphones have taken on new meanings. They have become markers of pandemic timelines ('before …', 'during …'). For some, such photos may include an image of the last gig attended before the 'lockdown' (here's to you, Hawthorne Heights!) which is now tainted by the sadness of what has since ensued. For others (including myself), they may find that the last picture of someone who has not survived the pandemic stands out and offers some solace. It is not only images on such phones that have been transformed into remnants of 'life before the pandemic' or part of a patchwork of memories of people.

Notes, messages, and other traces of time spent, that are stored on these devices, may be causing people to pause and ponder over how life has changed since then. What was any notion of 'normality' like for such people before the pandemic, and how might their phones have captured or (re)presented this in ways that these individuals are grappling with?

I write these words from 'a place of grief, restlessness, pain, peace, and remembrance for words, food, time, and love shared with specific people' (Sobande, 2021c). People's experiences of remembering can be, but are not always, healing. To what extent, if at all, can apps and functions such as Notes and Memories helpfully contribute to how people reflect on memories right now? In what ways may such apps and functions infringe on people's privacy and hamper their work to heal and hopes of remembering in ways that bring comfort, clarity, and maybe peace?

Smartphones are certainly more than just manufacturers of mirages of memories, and it would be disingenuous of me to suggest that I have not experienced numerous moments of joy from how I have connected, communicated, created, and cogitated with others via such devices. However, while corporations such as Apple continue to attempt to replicate the beauty of aspects of memory-making and remembering, and in doing so, distort the agentic, spontaneous, and uncapturable qualities of what it can mean to remember, smartphones remain sites of self-reflection and struggle, which include people's efforts to reflect on the past on their own terms. Speaking of the topic of reflection and struggle, the next section of this chapter discusses the animating force of forms of angst, such as by considering the generative nature of critique of the UK government's 'Eat Out to Help Out' scheme.

'EAT OUT TO HELP OUT' AND THE ANIMATING FORCE OF ANGST

On 8 July 2020, Chancellor of the Exchequer Rishi Sunak (who in 2022, was campaigning in an attempt to become Prime Minister) announced the UK's 'Eat Out to Help Out' discount scheme, to encourage people to dine outside of their homes to support the economy (and the nation). As is stated on the UK

Parliament website, the scheme 'was one of the Government's policy measures aimed to support businesses reopening after the COVID-19 lockdown period' (Hutton, 2020), and '[u]nder the Scheme Government provided 50% off the cost of food and / or non-alcoholic drinks eaten-in at participating businesses UK-wide. It applied all-day Monday to Wednesday from 3 to 31 August 2020. The discount is capped at a maximum of £10 per head' (ibid.).

During his announcement of the 'Eat Out to Help Out', scheme, as is documented in a recording on *The Telegraph's* (2020) YouTube channel, Sunak spoke of the intention to 'get customers back into restaurants, cafes, and pubs, and protect the 1.8 million people who work in them'. Sunak emphasized that such people working in the industry 'need our support', and that with this announced measure 'we can all eat out to help out'. The scheme seemed to be the spawn of both a capitalist market logic and the elastic language of social responsibility, such as in the form of calls to 'buy' and 'eat' local. The 'do good' tone of such discourse was dependent on ideas about being a 'good' and dutiful citizen, which are based on consumption (and economic (re)production) being equated with contributing to British society.

When Sunak referred to people working in 'restaurants, cafes, and pubs', who 'need our support', the message was that such support should take the form of the British nation eating out more, despite the prevalence of a highly contagious virus, and despite the fact that the government could have provided more support that would not have required calling on 'customers' to 'eat out to help out'. By placing the responsibility of sustaining this sector on the shoulders of 'customers', the UK government seemed to, at least rhetorically, absolve themselves of their own responsibilities related to this.

At the time that the 'Eat Out to Help Out' scheme was launched there were a range of reactions, which included critiques of the potential for the scheme to encourage in-person socializing that could result in a rise in COVID-19 cases. Other concerns expressed included worries about whether staff in this sector would be provided with the necessary resources and support to ensure their safety while at work. Some of these critiques were dismissed as nothing more than 'pearl-clutching' by individuals and groups hellbent on dismissing the existence and / or severity of coronavirus. In fact, some of such concerns were written off in ways that pathologized people's angst and (re)presented their perspectives as unreasonable, and, even, selfish. Moreover, in the context of Scotland, in addition to elsewhere in the world, '[d]espite the relatively small population of Black people, levels of incarceration – particularly within younger age groups – and detention under the mental health act, are disproportionate' (Sobande and hill, 2022: 141). Put frankly, the pathologization of people is a process that is raced, classed, gendered and impacted by a range of intersecting inequalities (Linton and Walcott, 2022).

It is beyond the objectives of this book to provide an in-depth discussion and analysis of how experiences of angst have been treated, depicted, and dismissed during the COVID-19 crisis. That said, I could not write this book without dedicating at least part of it to dealing with angst, including its animating force and the role that it can play in individual and collective struggles to survive. Although I use the example of angst in response to the 'Eat Out to Help Out' campaign as an entry point to this discussion, there are many examples of the UK government's (in)decisions that have contributed to people's experiences of angst during the COVID-19 pandemic (as well as before it).

As someone who can (and does) speak about angst at length, and as a 31-year-old who will likely never 'grow out' of their 'emo phase', I have a lot of thoughts on the ways that discourse on angst has been directed and discarded during the COVID-19 crisis, but in the interest of the word count of this book, I will keep them fairly brief. Sure, there are many different forms and experiences of angst (and angst can be severely debilitating, as well as being part of clinical diagnoses), but angst can also be an animating force that is part of how people make sense of societal risks and harms, as well as being part of how people refuse the ruse of rhetoric and representations that form political messaging that is intended to subdue dissent.

Too often angst is regarded as nothing other than inherently harmful and negative, which is a perception that I believe plays into the narratives of institutions that seek to sedate critique, including by marketing products and services to help people to 'self-soothe' (e.g., the 'keep calm and consume' overtones of some marketing messages during the COVID-19 crisis). Maybe as a 'nineties kid' who is still enthralled by the angst that gave us grunge, and a string of subcultures that followed, I am naively putting my hopes in the potential for angst to animate and breathe life into collective struggles. Or, maybe I'm just still riding the high of having recently seen *The Batman* (2022) (my third cinema experience in three years) which was a film that was as angsty as my emo heart had hoped for.

Whatever the reason, I am inclined to bring angst into this conversation about commodification and care during the COVID-19 crisis. Dictionary definitions are decidedly brief and such explanations never completely capture the breadth of interpretations of words and their many meanings. Despite this, dictionary definitions are often treated as indisputable facts rather than snapshots of understandings and impressions of words at specific points in time. Although dictionary definitions are sometimes contested, many are widely accepted in society. This means that such definitions and their circulation have the power to shape people's perception of words, and, consequently, perhaps their perception of the world. Hence, the need to critically consider how words are defined in dictionaries, and the extent to which such definitions do (or do not) encompass the multifaceted nature of words.

When writing about, and, riffing off ruminations on angst, I found myself flicking through the pages of dictionaries to identify the different ways they define it. The Cambridge Dictionary definition of angst is one of many explanations that I encountered: 'strong worry and unhappiness, especially about personal problems'. A slightly more nuanced definition is offered by Merriam-Webster which refers to angst as being 'a feeling of anxiety, apprehension, or insecurity'. Definitions such as the following include a focus on the forms of self-questioning that can be a part of angst, which involves a 'strong feeling of worry about what you should do, how you should behave or what will happen in the future' (Macmillan Dictionary, 2021).

Although angst is a term associated with acute experiences of inner turmoil, and intense forms of uncertainty, I argue that angst can play a powerful part in collective care work and forms of connection that may be essential to survival, and even, essential to experiencing joy. Despite the term angst typically being used to describe people's response to what they fear, angst can also be understood as sitting side by side with forms of agitation that are crucial to efforts to disrupt the oppressive status quo, such as by supporting socio-political movements that challenge structural inequalities.

Contrary to state efforts to reframe angst as nothing other than an individualized matter of mental health issues, angst and its arresting impact is sometimes a reminder of who and what you care about and just how much you do care, but in making this point I want to make clear that no two experiences of angst are the same. Also, although I recognize the capacity for angst to animate different expressions of care and collective efforts to facilitate it, I do so while emphasizing that angst is not something that should be romanticized or fetishisized – nor is it something that should be regarded as purely being experienced on an emotional or physical level.

When institutions appear to be committed to coaxing people into a state of numbness, denial, or cognitive dissonance to avoid critique, angst can be an anchor to reality that aids the rebuking of such efforts and re-energizes community work to take care of each other. For these reasons, for me, angst and hope often work in tandem, which is why marketing messages with placating tones during times of crises do little to assuage concerns or to bolster conviction in the brands behind such messaging.

If experiencing angst during times of crisis (which include the everyday experiences of many people both before and during the COVID-19 pandemic) is 'abnormal', what does that say about notions of 'normality' (and expectations of numbness that may be part of them)? Thinking about this question, in the final section of this chapter I take the opportunity to reflect once more on aspects of the relationship between ideas about 'normality', nostalgia, and time (before COVID-19). However, first, and shaped by the work of scholars Emma Casey and Jo Littler (2021: 489) on 'the neoliberal refashioning of housework', in the penultimate section of Chapter 3 I turn my attention to how home-baking and its online aestheticization and beautification has been framed and understood during the COVID-19 crisis.

Specifically, what follows involves analysis of socio-political meanings and messages that relate to the rise of digital depictions and discussion of home-baking, domesticity, and allegedly 'doing nothing' during this time. In doing so, I consider the work that can be involved in appearing to rest and appearing to refuse pressures to be productive. Meaning, as part of these reflections, I also think about how concepts such as 'slow work', 'soft life', and 'downtime' function in ways that are often fundamentally rooted in respectability politics and the experiences of people with the financial (and familial) resources that enable them to turn away from the pressures of productivity, and in some cases, enable them to perform (and even profit from) such a 'turning away' online.

BANANA BREAD'S 'MOMENT' AND THE CLASS POLITICS OF AESTHETICS OF 'EASE'

Particularly during the 'early days' of the COVID-19 crisis, digital discourse which documented people's experiences of domesticity during this time included many depictions and discussion of food. 'For those who lacked the confidence or fungus required of a sourdough starter, banana bread offered a simple alternative' (O'Connell, 2021: 561). In early 2021, banana bread was identified as having been the most Googled recipe at various points during the pandemic. From TikTok to Twitter – pictures and videos of freshly baked goods became one of many aspects of the online aesthetics that came to define certain – but, importantly, *not all* – experiences of domestic life during the crisis.

Scholars such as Stephanie Baines (2020) have commented on the connection between social media and banana bread becoming an Instagrammable pandemic 'baking trend'. In the words of Baines (2020), '[o]ur food preferences, acceptance and consumption are shaped by family and friends, advertising, celebrity trends and, these days, social media influencers'. I would add to that, they are also shaped by the racial and class politics of consumer culture. Informed by observations such as those of Baines (2020), I reflect on what a societal impulse to document baking during this time of crisis might reveal about discourses of productivity, their digital mediation and visibility, and raced, classed, and gendered notions of 'rest' and 'leisure'.

While during this time of crisis, scholars such as Kaete O'Connell (2021) have been 'more interested in the way food sustains our sense of self and relation to the world around us', I find myself preoccupied with understanding how (re)presentations of food are connected to the politics of work, rest, and constructions and experiences of comfort. Relatedly, and although it is beyond the scope of this book, the media framing of the Queen's Platinum Jubilee pudding, and the competition that was part of it, is ripe with material to study when considering the nationalist, imperialist, and classist implications of how food is framed in society – including the creation, consumption, naming, and praise / or dismissal of it.

It would be inaccurate to suggest that everyone who turned to baking during the COVID-19 crisis did so in ways that involved documenting this online. It would also be misinformed to claim that home-baking during this time, or at any time, has solely been a feature of middle-class experiences of domesticity. However, I believe that what Gabe Bergado (2020), writing for *Vogue*, referred to as being 'The banana bread renaissance of the coronavirus pandemic', contains various dynamics concerning class, gender, race, social media, and consumer culture that are worthy of close inspection. Such dynamics are impacted by geo-cultural power relations and the exploitation and abuse of farmers who work as part of the banana industry which, as the *Fairtrade Foundation* state on their UK website, 'provides employment for thousands of people in Latin America, the Caribbean, Southeast Asia, and West Africa. It generates vital foreign exchange earnings that governments depend on to improve health, education, infrastructure and other social services'.

Indeed, sometimes '[q]uarantine baking is less about producing grocery store alternatives and more about developing at-home hobbies. It is also an important exercise in stress relief, as evidenced by the plethora of images accompanying the hashtags #anxietybaking and #procrastibaking on social media' (O'Connell, 2021: 561). However, in recent years, polished images of perfectly baked banana bread have featured alongside statements and hashtags on social media that undoubtedly gesture towards an aspirational lifestyle of so-called 'rest', which is predicated on material conditions that are inaccessible to many people – particularly Black, Asian, and other structurally minoritized people in low-paid and unpaid work, which include banana farmers.

At times, home-baking and its beautification during the COVID-19 crisis was framed as an indication of time spent away from work, and was even alluded to as evidence of an *unproductivity* that has tenuously been framed as somewhat feminist in nature. In other words, whether it was banana bread, cookies, or another sweet concoction – home-baking, and the way that images and footage of it circulated in digital spaces during the pandemic, symbolize how forms of productivity become positioned, and are sometimes experienced, as pleasurable past-times – in ways that complicate ideas about work, rest, online visibility, and what Odell (2019) has referred to as 'doing nothing'.

As the work of many scholars has highlighted, calls for more rest and a return to radical forms of self-and collective care feature as part of feminist politics – not to suggest that such calls ever completely departed from feminism. What banana bread's 'moment' came to symbolize during the pandemic, in various ways, connects to how forms of rest, leisure time, and the perceived refusal to respond to certain pressures to produce are coded as 'feminist' in nature.

Put differently, I'm tentatively thinking about what might be the digitally mediated, and often raced, gendered, and classed logic of 'I baked (and posted about it online), therefore I rested'. In addition to this, I am thinking of who and what exists beyond the content and captions of social media depictions of banana bread – specifically, in the words of the *Fairtrade Foundation*, '[r]eports about problems in the banana industry often highlight the incredibly challenging situation for workers: low wages, precarious employment, restrictions on the right to organise into groups and the handling of unhealthy and environmentally hazardous chemicals without adequate protection, to name a few'.

As Horgan (2021: 1–2) notes, '[t]he Covid-19 crisis has shown that risk of harm to health at work is not evenly distributed. While the lack of PPE, long hours, and offensively low pay that NHS workers faced received rightful condemnation, the risks faced by workers in the low-pay and low-protection service sector were less often remarked upon' – including the work of those in the supermarkets and shops where people got their bananas to bake their beautiful bread.

I don't say all this to merely moralize or shame anyone who made banana bread during the crisis – I did so several times. Instead, I highlight this as a way of thinking critically about how some calls to, and praise of, 'rest' (including certain experiences of domesticity and cis-heteronormative home-making) during this time of crisis operate in ways that ultimately stem from inherently middle-class positions – namely, the views of individuals who were able to bake banana bread but did not have to farm or sell the ingredients that formed the recipe.

As Casey and Littler (2022: 489) have highlighted, 'within neoliberal culture, housework is now often refashioned as a form of therapy for women's stressful lives: stresses that neoliberalism and patriarchy have both generated and compounded'. Informed by this, I regard the digitally mediated framing of banana bread and home-baking during the crisis as reflecting what Casey and Littler (2022) observe, in addition to being reflective of how depictions and discourses of predominantly white, middle-class, domesticity come to define what 'rest' and 'ease' is.

When conceptualizing these sticky matters of what might be deemed the unsavoury side of the symbolic value of banana bread during the COVID-19 crisis, I find it helpful to reflect on nuanced differences between housework. For example, when engaging with some of the many pieces of content depicting home-baking, it can be difficult to determine exactly who and what (from ingredients, equipment, money, and filters) was involved in the process. Consequently, there may be times when such home-baking, and the way that it does or does not constitute a form of productivity or rest, departs from what is typically regarded as 'housework'. Is baking banana bread and beautifying it housework, aesthetic labour, both or neither? Also, whose experiences and perceptions of work and rest tend to underpin potential answers to these questions?

Contrary to how rest is often discussed in media, public, and political life, and as has been highlighted by the work of many disability justice scholars and activists, rest is not experienced in universal ways, and it certainly is not simply a matter of choice. What I mean by that is that the ability to rest, and what constitutes rest, is always shaped by the intersections of forms of oppression, including, but not limited to, racism, sexism, classism, misogyny, Islamophobia, and homophobia.

Sure – to some, baking banana bread is a restful act, and I do not suggest otherwise. In agreement with Bergado (2020), I recognize that 'there's something cathartic about creating something delicious out of bananas that are getting overripe and gross (which are the suggested state for the baked good)'. However, when home-baking and its online aestheticization is embroiled with discourses of ease and the so-called 'soft life', this often involves uncritically equating digitally mediated expressions of predominantly white and middle-class domesticity with rest. This can take shape in ways that actively mask the forms of labour that are involved in baking and the documentation of it – including potential differences between the material conditions of those involved in varied aspects of the process of farming and mixing ingredients. Also, digital depictions and discourses concerning banana bread and home-baking sometimes appear to be interconnected with constructions of idealized femininity, and in particular, motherhood, in ways that unsettlingly point towards conservative and cis-heteronormative notions of family life and parenting.

As the work of scholars Ana Sofia Elias, Rosalind Gill, and Christina Scharff (2017) highlights, women are societally expected to undertake many forms of aesthetic labour. Informed by their work, I contend that there is scope to deem some of the beautified digital content that captures home-baking during the crisis as symbolizing an extension of such aesthetic labour, and as being part of what Casey and Littler (2022: 489) term 'gendered and racialized histories of domestic labour and the figure of the "housewife"'. Perhaps the expansiveness of societal demands of aesthetic labour (which are particularly, but far from exclusively, directed at women) include an expectation to cutify and perfect the aesthetic of food for social media, and in ways that connect to wider and changing relations between 'gender and aspirational labour in the digital culture industries' (Duffy, 2015, 2017).

Comfort baking during the crisis may have sated some people's yearning for food from their childhood or may have enabled some parents to bond with their children while making sweet treats that are laced with a hint of attainable luxury. Was banana bread's 'moment' indicative of how productivity prevailed during this time, or an expression of how *some* people rested? Perhaps it's 'just not that deep'. However, I continue to beg to differ. Beyond the mouth-watering images of home-baking are layers of dynamics between race, class, gender, and both perceptions and experiences of productivity and rest, that are a reminder of how dominant societal discourse on domesticity and comfort during the COVID-19 crisis was a site within which a predominantly white and middle-class perspective was promoted. Continuing to think about themes such as comfort, but segueing into a focus on nostalgia, I now make and take time to sit with the question of 'remember when?'.

REMEMBER WHEN?

Remember life before COVID-19?

This is a question that many brands, and institutions in general, have encouraged us to consider over the last couple of years.

Adverts have prompted people to reflect (with rose-tinted glasses) on life before the crisis, at the same time as conveying marketing messages that seem to 'define what ("normal") life is like in the UK during the pandemic *for everyone*' (Sobande and Klein, 2022: 13).

As the charismatic character Don Draper in *Mad Men* highlighted when successfully pitching to Kodak, nostalgia can move people (to purchase products and become loyal to brands). However, nostalgia is complex:

> The warmth of an inside joke and the chill of a memory so vivid that it warps any sense of distinction between the past and the present. Always in the air but never fully in the moment, nostalgia flits and flees like a leaf dancing in the wind. At once, both beautiful and painful ... nostalgia cannot simply be manufactured. Instead, nostalgia is something that manifests in moments in ways that can never be completely controlled, commanded, and commodified. Nostalgia can be nurtured, but it is also always somehow unruly. (Sobande, forthcoming, 2023)

Thus, even though nods to nostalgia and constructions of a carefree past can be central to the marketing of brands, in their haste to hint at 'times before', some simply heave up a haze of depictions that reframe reality in ways that warp it to sell their products and / or services.

Marketed (re)presentations of a picture-perfect life before the COVID-19 pandemic reflect much regarding who may have felt that their life was great before, and whose experiences of hardship which predate the crisis are societally disregarded. It is not that I think that getting angsty about the content of adverts is any sort of revolutionary act. Rather, there is much hidden in plain sight in the UK advertising and marketing landscape, and continued critical analysis of that can help to deepen understandings of the politics of consumer culture *and* crises. It is with belief in the generative nature of critically considering both the past and the present, that I now move on to Chapter 4, which is the concluding chapter of this meditation on consuming crisis.

4

THE FUTURE, IN BLOOM

Figure 4.1 Mauve, pink, and yellow tulips in Cardiff, Wales

What are the ingredients of a world where flowers and people grow?

Where might the future take 'us'?

What brings a world into bloom and enables care to flourish?

I write these words while welcoming the arrival of Spring, and at a point in my life (and the lives of many other people) still marked by much grief, but also grounded in love (cariad) which transcends this world. I write these words with an ever-evolving understanding of the complexities and enduringness of care, which will always evade the complete capture of capitalism. But, above all, I write these words not as a conclusion, but as a way of exhaling.

When I think about the future – what is near and distant – I often struggle to picture what it might involve. This fills me with both fear and hope. I fear that the future may be punctured by the problems of the past and the present, but, mostly, I hope that the future takes a form that may currently be unimaginable. I hold onto the potential of a future where both flowers and people grow, and where both are tended to in ways that exist beyond the confines of the current capitalist system and the cruelties of governments. I'm not sure what the ingredients of such a world might be, but I know that forms of collective care will, *surely*, be at the centre of it.

The greed of the twenty-first century marketplace is such that the concept of growth has increasingly been associated with harm and hoarding, rather than flourishing and sustainability. Necessary work that calls for degrowth, including by grassroots groups such as *Enough!*, has highlighted that 'there is enough for all of us if we choose to live differently. Together, we are enough! Together we can find ways to move through times of crisis and beyond'. Echoing such sentiments, my hopes for the future include a hope for the simultaneous degrowth of commercial activity and the growth of collectivism, care, and comfort.

As has been continually pointed out, '[w]e are standing over an abyss. Our climate is changing in ways that imperil us, our fellow animals, other forms of life, and the very Earth itself' (Miller, 2017: 1). I hope that the climate (in every sense of the word) of the future is conducive with the needs of all, including non-human entities which are often extracted from their natural environment and exploited as part of the current conditions and crises of the world. Tomorrow is never promised but another world is always possible, and collective strives towards liberation make such a future palpable and poised to (one day) fully bloom.

REFERENCES

Ahmed, S. (2004) *The Cultural Politics of Emotion*. Edinburgh: Edinburgh University Press.

Aronczyk, M. (2013) *Branding the Nation: The Global Business of National Identity*. Oxford: Oxford University Press.

Arzumanova, I. (2021) 'Tasteful bunkers: shades of race and "contamination" in luxury design sectors'. *Architecture_MPS* 19(1). doi: 10.14324/111.444.amps.2021v19i1.004.

Asda (2020) 'Appeal from Roger, Asda's CEO: we're all in this together' [video]. *YouTube*, 26 March. Available at: www.youtube.com/watch?v=xYpnUunaRdk (accessed 10 July 2020).

Babb, B. (2021) 'The post-pandemic productivity mirage'. *The Independent*, 8 December. Available at: www.independent.co.uk/news/business/business-reporter/post-pandemic-productivity-mirage-business-b1963720.html (accessed 21 July 2022).

Bailey, M. and Mobley, I.A. (2018) 'Work in the intersections: a Black feminist disability framework'. *Gender & Society* 33(1): 19–40. doi: 10.1177/0891243218801523.

Baines, S. (2020) 'You're not done with banana bread – a psychologist reveals all'. *The Conversation*, 20 October. Available at: https://theconversation.com/youre-not-done-with-banana-bread-a-psychologist-reveals-all-148370 (accessed 15 February 2022).

Banet-Weiser, S. (2018) *Empowered: Popular Feminism and Popular Misogyny*. Durham, NC: Duke University Press.

Bassel, L. and Emejulu, A. (2018) *Minority Women and Austerity: Survival and Resistance in France and Britain*. Bristol: Policy Press.

BBC (2021) *Is Uni Racist?* Available at: www.bbc.co.uk/programmes/p09dhr3f (accessed 21 July 2022).

Benjamin, R. (2019) *Race After Technology: Abolitionist Tools for the New Jim Code*. Cambridge, UK: Polity Press.

Bergado, G. (2020) 'A delicious look into the banana bread renaissance of the coronavirus pandemic'. *Vogue*, 17 April. Available at: www.vogue.co.uk/miss-vogue/article/banana-bread-coronavirus (accessed 21 July 2022).

Boohoo (2022) 'HERE'S TO 2022, HERE'S TO YOU' [video] *YouTube* , 26 January. Available at: www.youtube.com/watch?v=l9oUbwqMQRM (accessed 21 July 2022).

Breeze, M., Taylor, Y. and Costa, C. (eds.) (2019) *Time and Space in the Neoliberal University: Futures and Fractures in Higher Education*. Cham: Palgrave Macmillan.

Cambridge Dictionary (year unknown) 'Angst'. Available at: https://dictionary.cambridge.org/dictionary/english/angst (accessed 3 May 2022).

Campbell, L. (2021) 'Direct (in)action: state suppression of community organising'. *Bella Caledonia*, 14 July. Available at: https://bellacaledonia.org.uk/2021/07/14/direct-inaction-state-suppression-of-community-organising/ (accessed 3 June 2022).

Carrigan, M. (2021) 'Social media is reshaping universities' value systems in a scramble for likes and shares'. *Mark Carrigan*, 5 November. Available at: https://markcarrigan.net/2021/11/05/social-media-is-reshaping-universities-value-systems-in-a-scramble-for-likes-and-shares/ (accessed 22 July 2022).

Carrington, B. and McDonald, I. (eds) (2001) *'Race', Sport and British Society*. London: Routledge.

Carter, D. (2018) 'Black study'. In A. Johnson, R. Joseph-Salisbury and B. Kamunge (eds) *The Fire Now: Anti-Racist Scholarship in Times of Explicit Racial Violence*, pp. 38–43. London: Zed Books.

Casey, E. and Littler, J. (2022) 'Mrs Hinch, the rise of the cleanfluencer and the neoliberal refashioning of housework: scouring away the crisis?' *The Sociological Review* 70(3): 489–505.

Chambers, N. (2019) 'Sometimes clocks turn back for us to move forward: reflections on black and indigenous geographies'. *Canada and Beyond: A Journal of Canadian Literary and Cultural Studies* 8(2019): 22–39.

Chatzidakis, A. and Littler, J. (2022) 'An anatomy of carewashing: corporate branding and the commodification of care during

Covid-19'. *International Journal of Cultural Studies* 25(3-4): 268–286.

Chatzidakis, A., Hakim, J., Littler, J., Rottenberg, C. and Segal, L. (2020) 'From carewashing to radical care: the discursive explosions of care during Covid-19.' *Feminist Media Studies* 20(6): 889–895.

Chen, M.Y. (2014) 'Brain fog: the race for cripistemology'. *Journal of Literary & Cultural Disability Studies* 8(2): 171–184.

Clarke, D.W. (2020) 'First my dad, then my iPhone: an autoethnographic sketch of digital death'. *Forum Qualitative Sozialforschung / Forum: Qualitative Social Research,* 21(2).

Collins Dictionary (2021) 'Normality'. Available at: www.collins dictionary.com/dictionary/english/normality#:~:text=Normality%20 is%20a%20situation%20in,work%20and%20shops%20 re%2Dopening (accessed 21 July 2022).

Cowan, L. (2021) *Border Nation: A Story of Migration.* London: Pluto Press.

Cowley, J. (2022) 'As a unified sense of British nationhood fades, we must ask: what is England?' *New Statesman,* 23 March. Available at: www.newstatesman.com/politics/uk-politics/2022/03/as-a-unified-sense-of-british-nationhood-fades-we-must-ask-what-is-england (accessed 25 March 2022).

Crenshaw, K. (1989) 'Demarginalizing the intersection of race and sex: a Black feminist critique of antidiscrimination doctrine, feminist theory and antiracist politics'. *University of Chicago Legal Forum* 1989(1): 139–167.

Crockett, D. (2021) 'Racial oppression and racial projects in consumer markets: a racial formation theory approach.' *Journal of Consumer Research* 49(1): 1–24.

Dabiri, E. (2022) 'Jay-Z and Beyoncé crossing a picket line to party shows how shallow celebrity activism really is'. *The Guardian,* 5 April. Available at: www.theguardian.com/commen tisfree/2022/apr/05/jay-z-beyonce-picket-line-party-celebrity-activism-oscars-chateau-marmont (accessed 21 July 2022).

Deliveroo (2021) 'We're England 'Til We Dine' [Video] *YouTube,* 2 June. Available at: www.youtube.com/watch?v=gKuAgrjX310 (accessed 21 July 2022).

Degot, E. and Riff, D. (eds) (2022) *There is No Society? Individuals and Community in Pandemic Times*. Cologne: Verlag der Buchhandlung Walther Konig.

Disney Channel UK (2020) 'Keep Your Spirits High ❤ | We're All in This Together | Disney Channel UK' [video]. *YouTube*, 8 June. Available at: www.youtube.com/watch?v=OpbfRNud8PQ (accessed 10 July 2020).

Dowell, E. and Jackson, M. (2020) '"Woke-washing"' your company won't cut it'. *Harvard Business Review*, 27 July. Available at: https://hbr.org/2020/07/woke-washing-your-company-wont-cut-it (accessed 21 July 2022).

Dowling, E. (2021) *The Care Crisis: What Cause it and How Can We End it?*. London and New York: Verso.

Drapers, G.W. (2020) 'Boohoo announces independent review following allegations of labour exploitation and dangerous working conditions in its UK supply chains'. *Business & Human Rights Resource Centre*, 8 July. Available at: www.business-humanrights.org/en/latest-news/boohoo-announces-independent-review-following-allegations-of-labour-exploitation-and-dangerous-working-conditions-in-its-uk-supply-chains/ (accessed 21 July 2022).

Duffy, B.E. (2015) 'The romance of work: gender and aspirational labour in the digital culture industries'. *International Journal of Cultural Studies* 19(4): 441–457.

Duffy, B.E. (2017) *(Not) Getting Paid to Do What You Love: Gender, Social Media, and Aspirational Work*. New Haven and London: Yale University Press.

Duffy, B.E. and Hund, E. (2019) 'Gendered visibility on social media: navigating Instagram's authenticity bind'. *International Journal of Communication* 13(2019): 4983–5002.

Elias, A.S., Gill, R. and Scharff, C. (eds) (2017) *Aesthetic Labour: Rethinking Beauty Politics in Neoliberalism*. London: Palgrave Macmillan.

Emejulu, A. and Bassel, L. (2015) 'Minority women, austerity and activism'. *Race & Class* 57(2): 86–95.

Emejulu, A. and Bassel, L. (2018) 'Austerity and the politics of becoming'. *Journal of Common Market Studies* 56(S1): 109–119.

Enough! (year unknown) 'Home'. Available at: www.enough.scot/ (accessed 10 May 2022).

Fairtrade Foundation (year unknown) 'Banana farmers and workers'. *Fairtrade Foundation*. Available at: www.fairtrade.org.uk/ farmers-and-workers/bananas/ (accessed 10 June 2022).

Feiner, J.R., Severinghaus, J.W. and Bickler, P.E. (2007) 'Dark skin decreases the accuracy of pulse oximeters at low oxygen saturation: the effects of oximeter probe type and gender'. *Anesthesia and Analgesia* 105(6): S18–S23.

Fitbit (2020) 'We're all in this together' [video]. *YouTube*, 13 April. Available at: www.youtube.com/watch?v=ub5ubZCmL4g (accessed 10 July 2020).

Gender Pay Gap App (2022) 'About the gender pay gap bot'. Available at: https://genderpaygap.app/ (accessed 21 July 2022).

Get Out (2017) [Film] Directed by Jordan Peele. Blumhouse Productions.

Gonsalves, G. and Kapczynski, A. (eds) (2020) *The Politics of Care: From COVID-19 to Black Lives Matter*. Cambridge, MA: Boston Review and Verso Books.

Glenday (2021) 'Deliver brand campaign unites the world behind effortless food'. *The Drum*, 5 April. Available at: www.thedrum. com/news/2022/04/16/deliveroo-brand-campaign-unites-the-world-behind-effortless-food (accessed 21 July 2022).

Glissant, É. (1997) *Poetics of Relation*. Ann Arbor: University of Michigan Press.

Gordon, L.R. (2022) *Fear of Black Consciousness*. London: Allen Lane.

Grier, S.A. and Poole, S.M. (2021) 'Will social marketing fight for Black lives? An open letter to the field'. *Social Marketing Quarterly* 26(4): 378–387.

Hall, S. (ed.) (1997a) *Representation: Cultural Representations and Signifying Practices*. Thousand Oaks, CA: SAGE.

Hall, S. (1997b) *Stuart Hall: Representation & the Media: Featuring Stuart Hall* [Media Education Foundation Transcript]. Available at: www.mediaed.org/transcripts/Stuart-Hall-Representation-and-the-Media-Transcript.pdf (accessed 21 July 2022).

Halpin (2020) *UK Universities' Response to Black Lives Matter*. Halpin, November. Available at: https://halpinpartnership.com/

wp-content/uploads/2021/09/Halpin-Report-UK-Universities-Response-to-Black-Lives-Matter.pdf (accessed 21 July 2022).

Hesse, B. (ed) (2000) *Un/Settled Multiculturalisms: Diasporas, Entanglements, Transruptions*. London: Zed Books.

hooks, b. (1992) *Black Looks: Race and Representation*. New York: Routledge.

Horgan, A. (2021) *Lost in Work: Escaping Capitalism*. London: Pluto Press.

Hutton, G. (2020) 'Eat Out to Help Out scheme'. *House of Commons Library*, 22 December. Available at: https://common slibrary.parliament.uk/research-briefings/cbp-8978/ (accessed 10 February 2021).

James, W. and Harris, C. (eds) (1993) *Inside Babylon: The Caribbean Diaspora in Britain*. London: Verso Press.

Jiménez-Martínez, C. (2021) *Media and the Image of the Nation during Brazil's 2013 Protests*. Cham: Palgrave Macmillan.

Johnson, A. (2018) 'An academic witness: white supremacy within and beyond academia'. In A. Johnson, R. Joseph-Salisbury and B. Kamunge (eds) *The Fire Now: Anti-Racist Scholarship in Times of Explicit of Racial Violence*, pp. 15–25. London: Zed Books.

Johnson, A. (2020) 'Covid-19 and cancer: following Audre Lorde'. *Feminist Review*. https://femrev.wordpress.com/2020/03/31/covid-19-and-cancer-following-audre-lorde/ (accessed 22 July 2022).

Johnson, A., Joseph-Salisbury, R. and Kamunge, B. (eds) (2018) *The Fire Now: Anti-Racist Scholarship in Times of Explicit Racial Violence*. London: Zed Books.

Johnson, G.D., Thomas, K.D., Harrison, A.K. and Grier, S.A. (eds) (2019) *Race in the Marketplace: Crossing Critical Boundaries*. Cham: Palgrave Macmillan.

Jones, N. (2021a) 'Digging deep where ritual, art, and ecologies meet'. *Naya Jones*. Available at: www.nayajones.com/ (accessed 22 July 2022).

Jones, N. (2021b) 'Prologue: Black dream geographies'. *Transactions of the Institute of British Geographers* 46(4): 825–828.

Jones, N. (2022) 'Black Dreaming and Black Dream Geographies'. *The Arrow*. Available at: https://arrow-journal.org/call-for-submissions/ (accessed 14 July 2022).

Joseph, R.L. (2018) *Postracial Resistance: Black Women, Media, and the Uses of Strategic Ambiguity.* New York: New York University Press.

Kamunge, B., Joseph-Salisbury, R. and Johnson, A. (2018) 'Changing our fate in the fire now.' In A. Johnson, R. Joseph-Salisbury and B. Kamunge (eds) *The Fire Now: Anti-Racist Scholarship in Times of Explicit Racial Violence,* pp. 1–12. London: Zed Books.

Kanai, A. and Gill, R. (2020) 'Woke? Affect, neoliberalism, marginalised identities and consumer culture'. *New Formations: A Journal of Culture/Theory/Politics* 102: 10–27.

Kay, J.B and Wood, H. (2020) 'Cultural commons: Critical responses to COVID-19, part 2'. *European Journal of Cultural Studies* 23(6): 1019–1024.

Kelley, W.M. (1962) 'If you're woke you dig it'. *The New York Times,* 20 May. Available at: www.nytimes.com/1962/05/20/archives/if-youre-woke-you-dig-it-no-mickey-mouse-can-be-expected-to-follow.html (accessed 22 July 2022).

Lawson, F. (2022) 'I was fed up with companies using International Women's Day to brag – so I set up a Twitter bot to expose their pay gaps.' *Metro,* 14 March. Available at: https://metro.co.uk/2022/03/14/i-set-up-a-twitter-bot-to-expose-companies-pay-gaps-16272035/ (accessed 22 July 2022).

Lewis, C., Regis, T. and Ofori-Addo, G. (2021) 'Sociological podcasting: radical hope, care and solidarity in a time of crisis'. *Soundings* 21(79): 94–109.

Linton, S. and Walcott, R. (2022) *The Colour of Madness: Mental Health and Race in Technicolour.* London: Bluebird.

Lorde, A. (1988) *A Burst of Light, Essays.* London: Sheba Feminist Publishers.

Littler, J. (2008) *Radical Consumption: Shopping for Change in Contemporary Culture.* Maidenhead: Open University Press.

Lovett, L. (2021) 'FDA warns pulse oximeters less accurate for people with darker skin'. *Mobi Health News,* 22 February. Available at: www.mobihealthnews.com/news/fda-warns-pulse-oximeters-less-accurate-people-darker-skin (accessed 22 July 2022).

Lury, C. (2004) *Brands: The Logos of the Global Economy.* London: Routledge.

Maclaran, P., Stevens, L. and Kravets, O. (eds) (2022) *The Routledge Companion to Marketing and Feminism*. London and New York: Routledge.

Macmillan Dictionary (year unknown) 'Angst'. Available at: www.macmillandictionary.com/dictionary/british/angst (accessed 10 March 2022).

Manzoor-Khan, S. (2022) *Tangled in Terror: Uprooting Islamophobia*. London: Pluto Press.

Marks & Spencer (M&S) (2020) 'We're all in this together' [video]. *YouTube*, 3 April. Available at: www.youtube.com/watch?v=VhzjqsRvC40&t=4s (accessed 10 July 2020).

Merriam-Webster (year unknown) 'Angst'. Available at: www.merriam-webster.com/dictionary/angst (accessed 3 February 2022).

McGonagle, E. (2020) 'Dettol's back to work ad goes viral for all the wrong reasons'. *Campaign*, 3 September. Available at: www.campaignlive.co.uk/article/dettols-back-work-ad-goes-viral-wrong-reasons/1693406 (accessed 22 July 2022).

McMillan Cottom, T. (2022) 'We're all "experts" now. That's not a good thing'. *The New York Times*, 10 January. Available at: www.nytimes.com/2022/01/10/opinion/scams-were-all-experts.html (accessed 22 July 2022).

Miller, T. (2017) *Greenwashing Culture*. London: Routledge.

Milton, J. (2022) 'Desperate Rishi Sunak wages war on "woke nonsense" and the Equality Act'. *Pink News*, 30 July. Available at: www.pinknews.co.uk/2022/07/30/rishi-sunak-trans-rights-equality-act/ (accessed 31 July 2022).

Mogaji, E. (2018) *Emotional Appeals in Advertising Banking Services*. Bingley: Emerald.

Mukherjee, R. and Banet-Weiser, S. (eds) (2012) *Commodity Activism: Cultural Resistance in Neoliberal Times*. New York: New York University Press.

O'Connell, K. (2021) 'Breadlines and banana bread: rethinking our relationship with food in the age of Covid-19'. *Diplomatic History* 45(3): 556–563.

Odell, J. (2019) *How to Do Nothing: Resisting the Attention Economy*. London and Brooklyn: Melville House.

Orgad, S. and Gill, R. (2022) *Confidence Culture*. Durham, NC: Duke University Press.

Pablo (2021) England 'Til We Dine: Deliveroo's new Euro's 2021 campaign. *Pablo.* Available at: www.pablolondon.com/work/england-til-we-dine (accessed 22 July 2022).

Piepzna-Samarasinha, L.L. (2018) *Care Work: Dreaming Disability Justice.* Vancouver: Arsenal Pulp Press.

Preece, C., Kerrigan, F. and O'Reilly, D. (2019) 'License to assemble: theorizing brand longevity'. *Journal of Consumer Research* 46(2): 330–350.

Rhodes, C. (2021) *Woke Capitalism: How Corporate Morality is Sabotaging Democracy.* Bristol: Bristol University Press.

Robinson, C.J. (1983) *Black Marxism: The Making of the Black Radical Tradition.* London: Zed Books.

Rosa-Salas, M. and Sobande, F. (2022) 'Hierarchies of knowledge about intersectionality in marketing theory and practice'. *Marketing Theory* 22(2): 175–189.

Ross, C. (2020) 'Millions are more productive while working from home, study finds'. *The Independent,* 17 September. Available at: www.independent.co.uk/life-style/work-from-home-productivity-talk-talk-coronavirus-b466148.html (accessed 22 July 2022).

Rossi, E. and Táíwò, O.O. (2020) 'What's new about woke racial capitalism (and what isn't): "wokewashing" and the limits of representation'. *Spectre,* 18 December. Available at: https://spectrejournal.com/whats-new-about-woke-racial-capitalism-and-what-isnt/ (accessed 22 July 2022).

Saha, A. (2012) 'Locating MIA: "race", commodification and the politics of production'. *European Journal of Cultural Studies* 15(6): 736–752.

Skeggs, B. cited in B. Skeggs, R. Hancock, A.H. Truong (2022) 'Care, with Bev Skeggs'. *The Sociological Review,* 22 April. Available at: https://thesociologicalreview.org/podcasts/uncommon-sense/care-with-bev-skeggs/ (accessed 22 July 2022).

Small, J. (2020) 'Will Dettol's "back-to-work" ad campaign damage its brand?' *Campaign,* 9 September. Available at: www.campaignlive.com/article/will-dettols-back-to-work-ad-campaign-damage-its-brand/1693790#:~:text=The%20short%20answer%20is%20no,same%20will%20be%20true%20here (accessed 22 July 2022).

Sobande, F. (2018a) 'Accidental academic activism'. *Journal of Applied Social Theory* [Online], 1.2 (2018): 83–101.

Sobande, F. (2018b) '*The "wokefluencers" of "diversity" marketing: the commercial co-optation of free(ing) online labour*', January, talk at After Work: Life, Labour and Automation symposium (University of West London).

Sobande, F. (2019) 'Femvertising and fast fashion: feminist advertising or *fauxminist* marketing messages'. *International Journal of Fashion Studies* 6(1): 105–112.

Sobande, F. (2020a) '"We're all in this together": commodified notions of connection, care and community in brand responses to COVID-19". *European Journal of Cultural Studies* 23(6): 1033–1037.

Sobande, F. (2020b) 'Woke-washing: "intersectional" femvertising and branding "woke" bravery. *European Journal of Marketing* 54(11): 2723–2745.

Sobande, F. (2020c) 'The revolution will not be branded'. *Disegno*, 10 June. Available at: https://disegnojournal.com/newsfeed/the-revolution-will-not-be-branded (accessed 22 July 2022).

Sobande, F. (2020d) 'Brands' optical "allyship" and opportunistic responses to Black social justice activism'. *Discover Society*, 1 July. Available at: https://archive.discoversociety.org/2020/07/01/brands-optical-allyship-and-opportunistic-responses-to-black-social-justice-activism/ (accessed 22 July 2022).

Sobande, F. (2020e) *The Digital Lives of Black Women in Britain.* Cham: Palgrave Macmillan.

Sobande, F. (2021a) '"Are we all in this together?": reflecting on a year of COVID-19 marketing messages'. *Developing Economics*, 27 April. Available at: https://developingeconomics.org/2021/04/27/are-we-all-in-this-together-reflecting-on-a-year-of-covid-19-marketing-messages/ (accessed 22 July 2022).

Sobande, F. (2021b) 'On beyond branding "brand activism" and whitewashing critiques of capitalism'. *Margins*, 14 November. Available at: https://marginstwenty.home.blog/2021/11/14/beyond-branding-brand-activism-and-whitewashing-critiques-of-capitalism/ (accessed 22 July 2022).

Sobande, F. (2021c) 'Cariad [Love]'. *Transactions of the Institute of British Geographers*, 46(4): 822–824.

Sobande, F. (2022a) 'On Black women's digitally mediated experiences of academia in Britain'. *Margins*, 29 May. Available: https://marginstwenty.home.blog/2022/05/29/on-black-womens-digitally-mediated-experiences-of-academia-in-britain/ (accessed 22 July 2022).

Sobande, F. (2022b) 'The celebrity whitewashing of Black Lives Matter and social injustices'. *Celebrity Studies* 13(1): 130–135.

Sobande, F. (2022c) 'Feeling at home at work?: Inequalities, inclusiveness, and changing work environments'. *Digit*, 5 July. Available at: https://digit-research.org/blog_article/feeling-at-home-at-work-inequalities-inclusiveness-changing-work/ (accessed 22 July 2022).

Sobande, F. and Emejulu, A. (2021) 'The Black feminism remix lab: on Black feminist joy, ambivalence and futures'. *Culture, Theory and Critique*. doi: 10.1080/14735784.2021.1984971.

Sobande, F. and Klein, B. (2022) '"Come and get a taste of normal": advertising, consumerism and the Coronavirus pandemic'. *European Journal of Cultural Studies*. doi.org/10.1177/13675494221108219.

Sobande, F. and Wells, J.R. (2021) 'The poetic identity work and sisterhood of Black women becoming academics'. *Gender, Work & Organization*. https://doi.org/10.1111/gwao.12747.

Sobande, F. and hill, l. (2022) *Black Oot Here: Black Lives in Scotland*. London: Bloomsbury.

Sobande, F. (forthcoming, 2023) 'Black media nostalgia in Britain'. *Cultural Studies*.

Sobande, F., Kanai, A. and Zeng, N. (2022) 'The hypervisibility and discourses of "wokeness" in digital culture'. *Media, Culture & Society*. doi.org/10.1177/01634437221117490.

Solidarity and Care (2020) 'About'. *Solidarity and Care*. Available at: www.solidarityandcare.org/ (accessed 22 July 2022).

Streeting, W. (2021) 'Only a Labour government will end child poverty. Let's make it happen'. *Labour List*, 19 May. Available at: https://labourlist.org/2021/05/only-a-labour-government-will-end-child-poverty-lets-make-it-happen/ (accessed 22 July 2022).

Tadajewski, M. (2011) 'Critical marketing studies'. In M. Tadajewski, P. Maclaran, E. Parsons and M. Parker (eds) *Key Concepts in Critical Management Studies*, pp. 83–87. London: SAGE.

Tadajewski, M. (2014) 'What is critical marketing studies? Reading macro, social, and critical marketing studies'. In R. Varey and M. Pirson (eds) *Humanistic Marketing*, pp. 39–52. London: Palgrave Macmillan.

Táíwò, O.O. (2022) *Elite Capture: How the Powerful Took Over Identity Politics (And Everything Else)*. London: Pluto Press.

Taylor, Y. and Lahad, K. (eds.) (2018) *Feeling Academic in the Neoliberal University: Feminist Flights, Fights and Failures*. Cham: Palgrave Macmillan.

The Batman (2022) [Film] Directed by Matt Reeves. Warner Bros.

The Care Collective (2020) *The Care Manifesto: The Politics of Interdependence*. London and New York: Verso.

The Drum (2021a) 'Deliveroo: England 'Til We Dine by Pablo'. *The Drum*, June. Available at: https://www.thedrum.com/creative-works/project/pablo-deliveroo-england-til-we-dine (accessed 22 July 2022).

The Drum (2021b) 'Halifax: It's a People Thing by New Commercial Arts'. *The Drum*, February. Available at: www.thedrum.com/creative-works/project/new-commercial-arts-halifax-its-people-thing (accessed 22 July 2022).

The Telegraph (2020) '"Eat out to help out" discount scheme announced by Rishi Sunak' [video]. *YouTube*, 8 July. Available at: www.youtube.com/watch?v=eIZ0Xhrvru4 (accessed 24 July 2020).

The Wall Street Journal (2020) 'Advertising in a pandemic: how brands are adjusting' [Video] *YouTube, 28 May*. Available at: www.youtube.com/watch?v=Q4DpxASLnXo (accessed 22 July 2022).

The Wheel (2007) *Mad Men*, Season 1, episode 13, AMC, 18 October.

Tyler, I. (2020) *Stigma: The Machinery of Inequality*. London: Zed Books.

University and College Union (UCU) (2021) 'Four fights dispute FAQS'. Available at: www.ucu.org.uk/article/11818/Four-fights-dispute-FAQs (accessed 22 July 2022).

Vredenburg, J., Kapitan, S., Spry, A. and Kemper, J.A. (2020) 'Brands taking a stand: authentic brand activism or woke washing?' *American Marketing Association* 39(4): 444–460.

Warren, D.E. (2022) '"Woke" corporations and the stigmatization of corporate social initiatives'. *Business Ethics Quarterly* 32(1): 169–198.

Who Cares? Scotland (2022) 'What we do'. Available at: www.whocaresscotland.org/ (accessed 21 July 2022).

INDEX